Achieving QTLS

The Minimum Core for
Numeracy
Audit and Test

Achieving **QTLS**

The Minimum Core for

Numeracy

Audit and Test

Mark Patmore and
Sarah Woodhouse

LearningMatters

First published in 2009 by Learning Matters Ltd

British Library Cataloguing in Publication Data
A CIP record for this book is available from the British Library.

ISBN 978 1 84445 272 9

Cover design by Topics – The Creative Partnership
Text design by Code 5
Project management by Deer Park Productions, Tavistock, Devon
Typeset by Pantek Arts Ltd, Maidstone, Kent
Printed and bound in Great Britain by Bell & Bain Ltd, Glasgow

Learning Matters Ltd
33 Southernhay East
Exeter EX1 1NX
Tel: 01392 215560
info@learningmatters.co.uk
www.learningmatters.co.uk

Contents

The authors

Mark Patmore is Senior Lecturer in mathematics education and Course Leader for the Mathematics Enhancement Programme in the School of Education at Nottingham Trent University. Mark is Principal Moderator for GCSE mathematics and Examiner for functional skills in mathematics. He was recently responsible for the mathematics input on the Level 4 Adult Numeracy Subject Specialist Courses provided by the university. He is also Examiner and External Verifier for a leading examination board for Skills for Life.

Sarah Woodhouse is Senior Lecturer in mathematics education in the School of Education at Nottingham Trent University. Previously, for several years, Sarah provided mathematics, statistics and numeracy support for students following a range of undergraduate courses at the university.

1

Why do trainee teachers need to meet the Minimum Core requirements?

The Minimum Core is a subject specification detailing the knowledge, understanding and personal skills in literacy, language (English) and numeracy (mathematics) expected of all teachers in the FE sector.

Evidencing the personal skills of literacy and numeracy is a mandatory element of the professional formation process of the Institute for Learning (IfL). This is the process that enables a teacher to gain licensed practitioner status, Qualified Teacher Status, Learning and Skills (QTLS) or Associate Teacher Status, Learning and Skills (ATLS).

The Further Education Teachers' Qualifications (England) Regulations 2007 state that no person may be employed in a teaching role unless they have either satisfied IfL that they have the necessary numeracy and literacy skills to teach or hold an award approved by the Secretary of State. These regulations apply to all those who entered teaching in the FE sector from 1 September 2007.

Section 2 Numeracy of the Minimum Core has two parts.

Part A is subdivided into two sections. Section A1 is concerned with the Personal, Social and Cultural factors influencing numeracy learning and development. Section A2 refers to the 'Explicit Knowledge of Numeracy Communication and Processes'. Part A is the subject of a companion book, *The Minimum Core for Numeracy: Knowledge, Understanding and Personal Skills* (Peart, 2009).

Part B deals with the personal Numeracy Skills. This book is concerned with Part B.

Note 1:
Evidence of personal skills in literacy and numeracy may have been acquired before the period of professional formation, or may be acquired within the time period allowed (up to five years from the commencement of the first contract in the sector). In either case evidence of personal skills is submitted during the professional formation period. A list of approved qualifications can be found on the Standards Verification UK (SVUK) web-site at **www.standardsverificationuk.org**. This list will be updated periodically to ensure that it remains fit for purpose. The following is a current list of acceptable qualifications for evidencing numeracy personal skills.

- Free Standing Maths Units – intermediate level.
- Key Skills Application of Number – Level 2 and above.
- National Numeracy Test Level 2.
- Functional skills in mathematics Level 2.
- Certificates in Essential Skills (3800).
- Northern Ireland Level 2 Certificate in Essential Skills – Application of Number.
- Core Skills numeracy – Intermediate 2 and above (Scottish NQ).
- GCSE mathematics A*–C.
- O level and CSE grade 1 mathematics.
- Mathematics Intermediate Level 2 (Scotland).

Note 2:
Those teachers who have gained Qualified Teacher Status (QTS) have already evidenced Level 2 skills in numeracy and literacy as part of gaining QTS and so are not required to do so again.

REFERENCES AND FURTHER READING REFERENCES AND FURTHER READING

Peart, S. (2009) *The Minimum Core for Numeracy: Knowledge, Understanding and Personal Skills*. Exeter: Learning Matters.

2
Skills audit

Introduction

You need to consider that your personal skills in mathematics should address the con-
texts and personal skills demands you may have within any programme of study you are
following and be informed by any initial assessment outcomes. A summative record of
minimum core coverage will be important for signposting to further professional development opportunities. The purpose of the audit is to allow you to establish what is
known, what is not known and what may be known either partially or with a degree of
uncertainty and so the audit provides a first step towards establishing a summative
record of coverage and together with the rest of the book will indicate those areas of
mathematics where you are confident and those where you need further consolidation
and/or guidance. However, any audit of a sensible length cannot cover all the content, as
will be seen from the table of coverage at the end of the audit.

It is difficult to identify the number of questions that must have been answered correctly
for a decision to be made about meeting the requirements of the minimum core.
Institutions and awarding bodies will need to assess the personal skill elements in line
with their overall assessment strategies and ensure that the personal skills developed are
the most appropriate for their trainees. As a guide – if you are unable to answer the
question or the majority of the questions in each category in this audit successfully you
are not meeting the requirements of the minimum core.

Note that almost all the questions require competence in basic arithmetic.

Q1 (Refer to Chapter 6)
(Example 1 in Chapter 6 provides a worked solution to this question)
This is a drawing of a classroom wall.
The shaded area will be used as a noticeboard.
What is the shaded area?

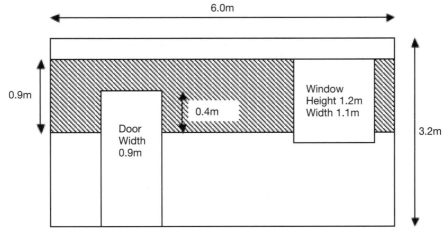

Answer: .... m²

Q2 (Refer to Chapter 6)

The shaded area you have calculated in Question 1 will be covered board ready to be used for display.

The board costs £13.50 per square metre plus VAT. Assume that the current rate of VAT is 17.5%. Using the answer from Question 1 find how much the board would cost, including VAT, to the nearest penny.

Answer: £................................

Q3 (Refer to Chapter 3)

A scale drawing of a classroom has a length of 170mm and a width of 120mm. If the scale is 1 : 50 what are the length and width of the room in metres?

Answer: Length .... m

Width .... m

Q4 (Refer to Chapters 3 and 6)

The layout of a classroom is shown below. There are 24 grey tables. Each table is square with a side length of 50cm.

The grey tables are moved to the side of the room.

The rest of the room can be used for practical work.

What is the ratio of the practical area to the area covered by tables? Write your answer in its simplest form.

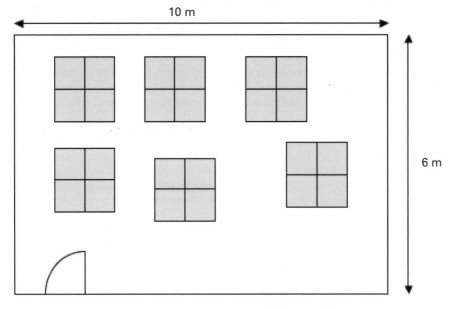

10 m

6 m

Answer: ratio = ...

Q5 (Refer to Chapter 3)

The maximum and minimum temperatures in a classroom are recorded on a thermometer.

The maximum temperature recorded is 18°C.

The minimum temperature recorded is 22°C lower.

What is the minimum temperature recorded?

Answer: ....°C

Q6 (Refer to Chapter 7)

Which of the following measures would be the most appropriate way of showing the difference between, for example, a maximum and a minimum temperature?

Mean, Median, Mode, Range, Standard Deviation.

Answer: ....

Q7 (Refer to Chapter 3)

This table shows part of the accounts for a college department:

Category	Annual budget (£)	Balance (£) at the end of the year
Books	2500	611
Photocopying	1750	−237
Consumables	950	239
Equipment	3750	−42

(a) How much was spent on photocopying?

Answer: ....

(b) Write down the names of any category where the actual expenditure is in excess of 75% of the budget.

Answer: ....

Q8 (Refer to Chapter 3)

The following table shows how a course is resourced for 12 students.
Complete the table to show what resources are needed for 15 students.

	For a class of 12	For a class of 15
Textbooks	8	
Stopwatches	4	
Name cards	12	
Reams of paper	16	

Q9 (Refer to Chapter 3)

A course is to be delivered in two-hour sessions on Wednesdays and Fridays. The tutor has been allocated 40 hours of contact time. The course will begin on Wednesday, 12 September. Use the following calendars to work out when it will finish. Holidays and weekends are shaded out.

September

M		3	10	17	24
T		4	11	18	25
W		5	12	19	26
T		6	13	20	27
F		7	14	21	28
S	1	8	15	22	29
S	2	9	16	23	30

October

M	1	8	15	22	29
T	2	9	16	23	30
W	3	10	17	24	31
T	4	11	18	25	
F	5	12	19	26	
S	6	13	20	27	
S	7	14	21	28	

November

M		5	12	19	26
T		6	13	20	27
W		7	14	21	28
T	1	8	15	22	29
F	2	9	16	23	30
S	3	10	17	24	
S	4	11	18	25	

December

M		3	10	17	24
T		4	11	18	25
W		5	12	19	26
T		6	13	20	27
F		7	14	21	28
S	1	8	15	22	29
S	2	9	16	23	30

Answer: ....

5

Q10 (Refer to Chapter 3)

(The example in Chapter 3, page 13, provides a worked solution to this question)

Photocopiers can enlarge or reduce originals.

The options for enlarging or reducing the size of originals are written as percentages on the photocopier display. These state how much larger, or smaller, each side of the drawing will become.

If an original is to be doubled in area which of the following options should be selected?

100%, 125%, 141%, 200%

Answer:.......................................

Q11 (Refer to Chapter 3)

Estimate the cost of photocopying 785 sheets at 2.05p each.

Answer:.......................................

Q12 (Refer to Chapter 7)

(Example 1 in Chapter 7 provides a worked solution to this question)

A survey of leisure time and part-time work of students in a college is to be carried out. The sample size is to be approximately one-third of the student population. Which of the following methods would provide an appropriate sample?

(a) Pick from the registers those born on the 3rd, 6th, 9th etc. of each month.

(b) Pick every third student in the cafeteria.

(c) Ask for volunteers and pick one-third of them.

(d) Obtain an alphabetical list of all students and pick every third name.

Answer:.......................................

Q13 (Refer to Chapter 7)

A survey of leisure time and part-time work of students in a college has been conducted. The median values of the responses are recorded in the following table.

Activity	Median hours spent per week	
	Males	**Females**
Computer/internet	10	6.5
Shopping	2	6
Socialising	8	8
Sport/exercise	4.5	2.5
TV	7.5	7.5
Paid work	6.5	5

(a) Based on the values in this table, state whether you agree with the following statements, giving your reasons.

    (i)   The median time spent doing sport/exercise for males and females together is 3.5.

    (ii) Men and women spend at most 8 hours a week socialising.

    (iii) Most people in the survey spend 7.5 hours a week watching TV.

    (iv) On average, men shop for 4 hours a week less than women do.

    (v) Some women spend 2.5 hours a week doing sport.

(b) Make three valid comparisons between the activities of males and females based on these data.

(i) ....

(ii) ....

(iii) ....

Q14 (Refer to Chapter 7)

The responses to the 'paid work' question for one group of students were:

Female (hours per week)	11	12	9	7	8.5	11.5	2	8		
Male (hours per week)	9	10.5	3	6	12.5	0	9	11	6	12

What are the mean times per week for the females and the males (to the nearest half hour)?

Answer: Females ....

Males ....

Q15 (Refer to Chapter 3)

The following table is used to calculate the retention rates of three groups of students.

The retention rate is defined as the percentage of students who complete a course. Complete the table, giving your answers to one decimal place.

	Number of students at start of course	Number of students dropping out of course	Retention rate (%)
ICT	123	25	
Literacy	157	34	
Numeracy	132	27	

Q16 (Refer to Chapter 3)

A lecturer at Mid-England College is organising a visit to Berlin.

A German hotel offers accommodation for €45 for three nights. The exchange rate, when the hotel was booked, was £1 = €1.463.

What was the accommodation cost in pounds (£), to the nearest penny?

Answer:......................................

Q17 (Refer to Chapter 6)

The distance from Mid-England College to the ferry port is 270 miles.

The average speed for a coach for the journey, allowing for stops and delays, is 40 miles per hour.

(a) What is the expected length of the journey, in hours and minutes?

Answer: (a)......................................

The ferry will sail at 17.30 hours and boarding must be completed 30 minutes before this.

(b) What is the latest time to leave the college in order to be at the port in time? Give your answer in 24-hour clock time.

Answer (b):......................................

(c) Five miles is approximately 8 kilometres. What is the distance between the college and the port in kilometres?

Answer (c):......................................

Q18 (Refer to Chapter 8)
In Berlin students will be given a choice on the second day of an activity.
In the morning they have a choice between:
- a museum;
- a city tour;
- an art gallery.
In the afternoon they have a choice between:
- a zoo;
- a shopping centre;
- a cinema;
- a tour of a football stadium.
The choice of the morning activity does not affect the choice of the afternoon activity.
How many different combinations of activities are possible?

Answer:......................................

Q19 (Refer to Chapter 3)
Some students raise money for charity by collecting ring pulls from drinks cans. They receive £5 for every 1250 ring pulls collected, with a bonus of £10 for every 5000 ring pulls collected.
How much money do they raise if they collect 7500 ring pulls?

Answer:......................................

Q20 (Refer to Chapter 3)
Which is the greater amount?
0.7 times 70
two-thirds of 72
15% of 300
Show your working out.

Answer:......................................

Q21 (Refer to Chapter 4)
(The example in Chapter 4, page 23, provides a worked solution to this question)
A lecturer is checking on the current, in amps, of a new cooling fan for her classroom.
The fan has a power rating of 2100 watts. The voltage of the electrical supply is 240 volts.
Use the formula

Power (in watts) = voltage (in volts) × current (in amps)

to find the current, in amps, through the fan.
Give your answer to the nearest whole number.

Answer:......................................amps

Q22 (Refer to Chapter 3)
This is part of a chart showing the distance in miles between some places in England.

Birmingham										
Bristol	80									
Carlisle	199	282								
Dover	207	206	400							
Exeter	164	84	355	244						
Hull	134	231	170	264	305					
Leeds	116	212	126	271	286	60				
Lincoln	99	186	182	220	260	47	72			
Liverpool	102	184	126	304	258	128	74	140		
London	120	120	313	72	200	187	198	143	215	
Manchester	89	172	123	291	291	97	44	85	35	202
Nottingham	52	145	188	218	218	92	74	38	112	131	71
	Birmingham	Bristol	Carlisle	Dover	Exeter	Hull	Leeds	Lincoln	Liverpool	London	Manchester

Rob is a salesman. Use the chart to work out how far he travels if his journey is from Nottingham to Lincoln then to Carlisle then to Bristol and back to Nottingham.

Answer:..miles

Summary table for coverage of Minimum Core content

Use this table to indicate those questions you were successful in and those where you need further practice

Question Number	Number	Fractions, decimals, percentages	Ratio and proportion	Algebra	Shape, space and measures	Statistics	Probability
1					✓		
2	✓	✓			✓		
3			✓				
4			✓		✓		
5	✓						
6							✓
7	✓						
8	✓						
9	✓						
10			✓				
11	✓						
12						✓	
13						✓	
14						✓	
15		✓					
16	✓						
17	✓				✓		
18							✓
19	✓						
20		✓					
21				✓			
22	✓						

Conclusion

At the end of this audit you should now be able to judge the content area or the topics within an area that you feel confident with, what you feel unsure about and those about which you have no or very little knowledge. Working through the following chapters will provide you with more practice and increase both your knowledge and confidence.

3
Number

By the end of this chapter you should be able to:

- **use appropriate methods, operations and tools to explore a situation and solve problems;**
- **use appropriate reasoning, strategies and techniques to solve problems;**
- **apply appropriate knowledge of number and skills in number;**
- **assess your own level of understanding in the context of number.**

This chapter and its objectives contribute to the following Minimum Core requirements:
Part B: Personal Numeracy Skills: Processes.

This chapter also contributes to the following LLUK Standards:
AS4, AS7, AP4.2, BS2, CK1.1, CK1.2, CP1.1, CK3.4, CP3.4.

Introduction

This chapter provides you with an opportunity to check your understanding of the number knowledge and skills, which implicitly include arithmetic processes and operations, listed in the Minimum Core. Competence in this area is vital, for an inability to handle numbers will restrict progress in other content areas. The Minimum Core sets out that personal skills in numeracy include, amongst other things, *the ability to communicate about numeracy concepts, to develop one's own understanding of numeracy concepts and recognise and analyse misconceptions, (and misunderstandings).* The Minimum Core also states that you should be able to use a calculator efficiently, be able to estimate, approximate and check working. The contents of this chapter are intended to cover the list given below in the 'Links to the Minimum Core'. It is important that if you do have difficulty in understanding how to proceed with a question or if your answer is incorrect and you are unable to identify why, that you ask for help from the teaching staff of your institution or consult textbooks or GCSE revision guides.

Links to the Minimum Core:

The Minimum Core lists the following knowledge and skills for number:
- **understanding positive and negative numbers of any size;**
- **carrying out calculations with numbers of any size;**
- **understanding and using equivalences between fractions, decimals and percentages;**
- **calculating with fractions;**
- **calculating with percentages;**
- **calculating with decimals to a given number of decimal places;**
- **using and calculating with ratio and proportion.**

The importance of these topics may be inferred from the following examples of use in professional life and application in subject areas:

Concept	Examples
Understanding positive and negative of any size	<ul><li>Monitoring budget forecasts, actual expenditure</li><li>Monitoring room or laboratory temperature</li><li>Monitoring temperatures in refrigerators and freezers</li><li>Temperatures below freezing</li><li>Debt</li><li>Distance below sea level</li></ul>
Carrying out calculations with numbers any size (Note: this implies an understanding of place value and that the position of a digit signifies its value)	<ul><li>All types of numbers from the very large to the very small</li><li>Population figures</li><li>Financial calculations</li><li>Large numbers such as computer disk capacity and digital camera resolution</li><li>Government spending on e.g. education</li><li>Atom and molecule measurements</li><li>Comparing temperatures, prices and measurements</li><li>Interpreting calculator displays when very large or very small numbers are given in standard form</li></ul>
Understanding and using equivalences between fractions, decimals and percentages (Note: this implies an understanding of how to order numbers, fractions, decimals and percentages) Calculating: <ul><li>with fractions</li><li>with percentages</li><li>with decimals to a given number of decimal places</li></ul>	<ul><li>Money, measurement and capacity</li><li>Calculating areas and volumes using measurements in whole numbers, decimals and fractions</li><li>Class sizes, class marks and averages</li><li>Percentage attendance, retention and achievement</li><li>Calculating pay, pay increases and pension entitlement</li><li>VAT percentage increase or reduction</li><li>Finances, mortgage rates and investments</li><li>Identifying (and using) appropriate degrees of accuracy, e.g. two decimal places when working with money</li></ul>
Using and calculating with ratio and proportion	<ul><li>Staff/student ratios in classrooms</li><li>Scaling photocopies</li><li>Correct mixture proportions for hairdressing, catering, construction and horticulture</li><li>Currency exchange</li><li>Unit pricing</li><li>Compression ratios</li><li>Staff-to-client ratios in the care sector</li><li>Scaling quantities up or down</li><li>Proportion in art and design</li><li>Scale in maps and drawings</li></ul>

Implicit throughout is the ability to check both calculations, using for example, inverse operations, and the reasonableness of any answers using rounding, estimating and checking.

Further examples of how you would use these skills in professional life and application in subject areas include:

- **checking student work;**
- **costing;**
- **project funding;**
- **planning and drafting projects and bids;**
- **checking own or peer work;**
- **financial transactions;**
- **anticipating likely results;**
- **calculations in specific vocational areas;**
- **checking spreadsheet calculations;**
- **rounding numbers when drawing graphs and charts.**

HINTS AND TIPS

- Round up and down when estimating calculations so that to estimate the answer to 18.46×23.21 find the answer to 20×20 $(= 400)$.
- Ratio can occur in different situations:
  (i) with similar figures, where the ratio of corresponding sides or lengths is equal and the ratio of lengths is equal to a scale factor so that if a length is enlarged as might happen with a scale model then

  $$\frac{\text{enlarged length}}{\text{original length}} = \text{scale factor}$$

  (ii) with fractions and percentages so that if a group had 30 males and 40 females then

    – what is the ratio of males to females? Answer is 30 : 40 or 3 : 4

    – what fraction of the group are males? Answer is $\dfrac{30}{70} = \dfrac{3}{7}$

    – what proportion of the group are male? Answer is $\dfrac{30}{70} = \dfrac{3}{7}$

- To convert a fraction to a decimal divide the numerator by the denominator.
- To convert a decimal to a percentage multiply it by 100.
- Percent means 'out of 100' so 23% means 23 out of 100 or $\dfrac{23}{100}$.
- When asked to estimate, round all values to 1 significant figure before doing the calculation.
- To find a fraction or percentage of an amount, convert the fraction or percentage to a decimal and then multiply it by the amount.

EXAMPLE

Worked example:
(Skills Audit Question 10)

Photocopiers can enlarge or reduce originals.

The options for enlarging or reducing the size of originals are written as percentages on the photocopier display. These state how much larger each side of the drawing will become.

If an original is to be doubled in area which of the following options should be selected?

100%   125%   141%   200%

Notes

A square with a side length of 10cm has an area of 10cm × 10cm = 100cm².

Doubling the size of the square so that the side length = 20cm gives an area of 20 × 20cm = 400cm², i.e. 4 times bigger.

Working through other examples if necessary you can see that the ratio of the enlarged area to the original area = (the ratio of the new length to the original length)².

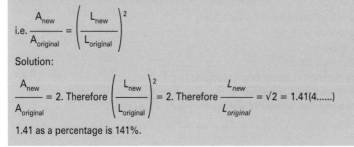

i.e. $\dfrac{A_{new}}{A_{original}} = \left(\dfrac{L_{new}}{L_{original}}\right)^2$

Solution:

$\dfrac{A_{new}}{A_{original}} = 2$. Therefore $\left(\dfrac{L_{new}}{L_{original}}\right)^2 = 2$. Therefore $\dfrac{L_{new}}{L_{original}} = \sqrt{2} = 1.41(4......)$

1.41 as a percentage is 141%.

Key information

Accuracy   is the degree of precision given in the question or required in the answer. For example, a length might be measured to the nearest centimetre, money could be quoted to the nearest pence while an average (mean) test result might be rounded to one decimal place.

Decimal   Decimals are numbers based on or counted in a place value system of tens. A decimal point is placed after the units digit in writing a decimal number, e.g. 1.25. The number of digits to the right of the decimal point up to and including the final non-zero digit is expressed as the number of decimal places. For 1.25 there are two digits after the decimal point, and the number is said to have two decimal places, sometimes expressed as 2 dp. Many simple fractions cannot be expressed exactly as a decimal. For example, the fraction $\frac{1}{3}$ as a decimal is 0.3333..... which is usually represented as $0.\dot{3}$ (i.e. 0.3 recurring). Decimals are usually rounded to a specified degree of accuracy, e.g. 0.6778 is 0.68 when rounded to 2 dp. 0.5 is always rounded up, so 0.5 to the nearest whole number is 1.

Fraction   Fractions are used to express parts of a whole, e.g. $\frac{3}{4}$. The number below the division line, the denominator, records the number of equal parts into which the number above the division line, the numerator, has been divided.

Percentage   A percentage is a fraction with a denominator of 100, but written as the numerator followed by '%', e.g. $\frac{25}{100}$ or 25%. Percentages can be used to compare different fractional quantities. For example, in mathematics class A, 10 students out of 25 are also studying further mathematics; in class B, 12 out of 30 students are studying further mathematics. However, both $\frac{10}{25}$ and $\frac{12}{30}$ are equivalent to $\frac{4}{10}$, or 40%.

Proportion   A relationship between two values or measures. These two values or measures represent the relationship between some part of a whole and the whole itself. See notes in 'Hints and Tips' above.

Ratio   A comparison between two numbers or quantities. A ratio is usually expressed in whole numbers. See notes in 'Hints and Tips' above.

Rounding   Expressing a number to a degree of accuracy. For example, it may be acceptable in a report to give outcomes to the nearest hundred or ten. So the number 774 could be rounded up to 800 to the nearest hundred, or down to 770 to the nearest ten. If a number is halfway or more between rounding points, it is conventional to round it up, e.g. 55 is rounded up to 60 to the nearest ten and 3.7 is rounded up to 4 to the nearest whole number. If the number is less than halfway, it is conventional to round down, e.g. 16.43 is rounded down to 16.4 to one decimal place.

Key questions

Q1 The maximum and minimum temperatures in a classroom are recorded on a thermometer.
The maximum temperature recorded is 23°C.
The minimum temperature recorded is 24°C lower.
What is the minimum temperature recorded?

Q2 This table shows part of the accounts for a college department.

Category	Annual budget (£)	Balance (£)
Books	3300	690
Photocopying	1570	−265
Consumables	850	318
Equipment	3250	−68

(a) How much was spent on photocopying?

(b) Write down the names of any category where the expenditure is in excess of 75% of the budget.

Q3 The following table shows how a course is resourced for 12 students.

Complete the table to show what resources are needed for 18 students.

	For a class of 12	For a class of 18
Textbooks	8	
Stopwatches	4	
Name cards	12	
Reams of paper	16	

Q4 Estimate the cost of photocopying 1234 sheets at 1.82p each.

Q5 The following table is used to calculate the retention rates of three groups of students. The retention rate is defined as the percentage of students who complete a course. Complete the table, giving your answers to one decimal place.

Number of students at start of course	Number of students dropping out of course	Retention rate (%)
ICT	223	37
Literacy	310	34
Numeracy	156	28

Q6 A lecturer is organising a visit to Berlin.
A German hotel offers accommodation for €56 to stay for three nights. The exchange rate is £1 = €1.22.
What is the accommodation cost in pounds (£), to the nearest penny?

Q7 Five miles is approximately 8 kilometres. Convert 568 miles into kilometres.

Q8 Some students raise money for charity by collecting ring pulls from drinks cans. They receive £4 for every 1250 ring pulls collected, with a bonus of £8 for every 4000 ring pulls collected.
How much money do they raise if they collect 5500 ring pulls?

Q9 Which is the greater amount?
0.7 times 70
two-thirds of 72
15% of 300

Q10 Look at the following calculations. Check to see if they are correct. If you judge them to be incorrect write down the correct answer

(i) 13.4 + 5   Answer is 13.9

(ii) John has a 4-hour videotape. He records a film lasting $2\frac{1}{2}$ hours and a programme lasting $\frac{3}{4}$ of an hour. How long is left on the tape?

Answer is $2\frac{1}{2} + \frac{3}{4} = 2\frac{2}{3}$ $4 - 2\frac{2}{3} = 1\frac{1}{3}$

(iii) 0.2 x 0.4   Answer is 0.8

(iv) Write down the number fifty-three-thousand four-hundred and seven
Answer is 53,000,407

Q11 Some Catering students have been given this recipe for strawberry ice-cream. The recipe is for 6 people.

> **Strawberry ice-cream**
>
> 600g strawberries
>
> 250g sugar
>
> 200ml cream
>
> 100ml water

(a) What weight of strawberries will they need to make ice-cream for 10 people?

(b) How much sugar will they need for 10 people?

Q12 This is a familiar logo.

The two logos are mathematically similar. The width of the smaller is 3.2 cm. The scale factor of the enlargement is 1.5.

(a) How wide is the larger?

The height of the larger logo is 4.7 cm.

(b) How high is the smaller?

Q13 For an end-of-term assessment, a group of students are producing a free college newsletter. It will be printed both sides on A4 size sheets of paper. As well as pictures each page will have space for about 320 words and there will be 8 pages.

There are already seven items with these word lengths:

Sports update	285 words
Letters	340 words
About the editorial team	28 words
Bullying survey	185 words
Revenue of recent drama	289 words
College news update	456 words
Comment	286 words

About how much space for words is still remaining for more items? Give your answer both as an estimate of words and the number of pages.

Q14 A noticeboard for a classroom is 4.5m by 1.5 m.

Board costs £13.50 per square metre plus VAT. Assume that the current rate of VAT is 15%. How much will the board cost, including VAT, to the nearest penny?

Q15 Catering students sell cream teas at a college open day. A cream tea costs £2.75.
They sell 88 cream teas and collect £242.
Which calculation should they use to check that this calculation is correct?

(a) $\dfrac{242}{88}$

(b) $\dfrac{275}{242}$

(c) $\dfrac{88}{2.75}$

(d) $\dfrac{275}{88}$

Q16 As part of a project some Business Studies students collect information about a small firm making parts for the motor industry.

The firm employs 469 men and 231 women. 176 of the employees are under 25.

(a) What is the approximate ratio of men to women employees?
(b) What is the proportion of women compared with the total work force?
(c) What fraction of the employees are under 25?

Q17 A college sports hall is available for hire. The costs are listed in the following table.

Sports hall Costs for private hire	
Monday to Friday (6 p.m. to 10 p.m.)	£25 per hour
Saturday (9 a.m. to 4 p.m.)	£45 per hour
Sunday (9 a.m. to 4 p.m.)	£50 per hour
Equipment hire	Flat rate charge of an extra £30 per booking
Deposit	15% of total cost

How much does it cost to hire the hall for three hours on a Saturday with equipment hire?

Q18 The manager of a cinema records the number of people attending the afternoon showing during one summer holiday week, from Monday to Friday.

Day of the week	Mon	Tues	Wed	Thurs	Frid
Number of adults	156	186	135	142	216
Number of children	44	89	52	62	98

(a) What was the ratio of the number of children to the number of adults? Give your answer in its simplest form.

(b) The following week the number of people had increased to 1350. What was the percentage increase in the number of people?

Tickets cost £6.50 for adults and £2.80 for children.

(c) What is the price of a child's ticket as a fraction of an adult's ticket?

Q19 A factory cleaner earns a basic rate of £11.20 per hour for a 35-hour week. For each hour over 35 hours he works he earns $1\frac{1}{4}$ times the basic rate.

(a) One week he works 40 hours. How much does he earn?

(b) His pay is increased by $2\frac{1}{2}$%. What is his new rate of pay per hour?

Q20 Hannah has been asked to produce a fruit drink for a summer fete.

She decides to experiment with a drink made from cranberries and sparkling (fizzy) water.

For her experiments she tries four different recipes.

Recipe A
2 glasses of cranberry juice
3 glasses of water

Recipe B
4 glasses of cranberry juice
8 glasses of water

Recipe C
3 glasses of cranberry juice
5 glasses of water

Recipe D
1 glass of cranberry juice
4 glasses of water

(a) Which recipe has the strongest cranberry flavour?

(b) Which recipe has the weakest cranberry flavour?

1 litre cartons of cranberry juice cost £1.85.
1.5 litre bottles of sparkling water cost £1.23.

For the glasses Hannah decides to buy 260ml plastic cups which cost £2.19 for a 100 pack.

She needs to make enough to be able to sell 240 cups of the mixture at the fete. How many cartons and bottles does she need to make 240 cups of the mixture from the recipe which gives the strongest cranberry flavour?

(c) How much will this cost?

(d) How much should she sell each cup for in order to make at least 5p profit per cup?

Q21 The maximum and minimum temperatures in a classroom are recorded on a thermometer.
The maximum temperature recorded is 26°C.
The minimum temperature recorded is 29°C lower.
What is the minimum temperature recorded?

Q22 *Tree Tea* tea bags cost £1.98 for a box of 80 and £1.28p for a box of 50.

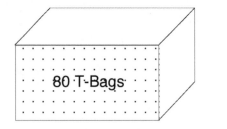 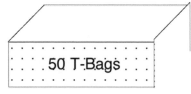

Which represents the best value?

Q23 Use your calculator to work out:

(a) $\dfrac{5.72 \times 4.92}{3.75 - 1.49}$

(b) $\dfrac{3 \times 4.6 \times 5.4^2}{4.6 + 5.4}$

(c) What rough calculations would you do to check your answer to (a) and (b)?

Q24 Use all of the digits 1, 3, 5, 7 to make two decimal numbers such that:

(a) the difference between these two numbers is less than 2.0

and

(b) the product of these two numbers is less than 6.0.

Q25 *Sodapeps* make canned drinks. Each can contains 440 ml. A new can is made to hold 500 ml.

(a) What is the percentage increase in the size of can?

The measurement 440 ml is correct to the nearest millilitre.

(b) What is the least amount the can could contain?

Q26 Harry wants to check his electricity bill for the period October to January.

He knows the following facts:

- one unit of electricity = 1 kilowatt hour (kWh);
- the first 242 kWh used are charged at 12.058p per kWh;
- the next kWh used are charged at 6.25p per kWh.

Calculate the amount Harry has to pay if the meter reading in October was 79994 units and in January was 81805 units.

Q27 There are three main food types: protein, fat and carbohydrate. The energy each provides is listed in the following table.

Food type	Energy provided per gram in kilocalories
Protein	4
Fat	9
Carbohydrates	4
Note: 1 kilocalorie is approximately equivalent to 4.2 kilojoules	

The amount of protein, fat and carbohydrate that Jan eats on Wednesday is shown below:

	Breakfast	Lunch	Dinner	Snacks
Protein (g)	22.5	37.8	42.4	11.8
Fat (g)	13.4	38.4	46.9	22.4
Carbohydrate (g)	135.0	78.0	200.4	13.5

(a) How many kilocalories of food are provided by the food Jan eats on Wednesday?

An active woman needs 10,500 kilojoules of energy each day.

(b) What is the difference in the number of kilojoules needed by an active woman and the number of kilojoules provided by the food Jan eats on Wednesday? Give your answer as a percentage of the active woman's needs.

The recommended amount of energy from fat is 35% of the total energy intake.

(c) Did Jan's energy input from fat meet the recommendation or not? Justify your answer.

A SUMMARY OF KEY POINTS

In this chapter you have learnt how to:

> **deal with numbers in different contexts;**

> **understand and use with confidence fractions, decimals, ratio and percentage;**

> **interpret and analyse information given in questions.**

REFERENCES AND FURTHER READING REFERENCES AND FURTHER READING

There are few books specifically targeted at number. Most GCSE textbooks written for the Higher tier of entry will cover the number content.
However, some useful sources of further reading at an appropriate level are:

Cooke, H., Houssart, J. and Mason, J. (2001) *Passport to Numeracy*. Buckingham: Open University Press.
Mooney, C., Ferrie, L., Fox, S., Hansen, A. and Wrathmell, R. (2009) *Primary Mathematics: Knowledge and Understanding*. (4th ed.) Exeter: Learning Matters.

Websites
www.nrich.maths.org.uk
www.cimt.plymouth.ac.uk
www.bbc.co.uk/gcsebitesize
www.bbc.co.uk/revision

4
Algebra

By the end of this chapter you should be able to:

- **use appropriate methods, operations and tools to explore a situation and solve problems;**
- **use appropriate reasoning, strategies and techniques to solve problems;**
- **apply appropriate knowledge of algebra and skills in algebra;**
- **assess your own level of understanding in the context of algebra.**

This chapter and the objectives contribute to the following Minimum Core requirements:
Part B: Personal Numeracy Skills: Processes

This chapter also contributes to the following LLUK Standards:
AS4, AS7, AP4.2, BS2, CK1.1, CK1.2, CP1.1, CK3.4, CP3.4.

Introduction

This chapter provides you with an opportunity to check your understanding of the algebra knowledge and skills, which implicitly include looking for and examining patterns and using notation accurately listed in the Minimum Core. The Minimum Core also states that you should be able to use knowledge of related problems and in this chapter there are clear, but implicit links to the number content. The Minimum Core sets out that personal skills in numeracy, (here algebra), include, amongst other things, *the ability to communicate about numeracy concepts, to develop one's own understanding of numeracy concepts and recognise and analyse misconceptions, (and misunderstandings).* The contents of this chapter are intended to cover the list given below in the 'Links to the Minimum Core'. It is important that if you do have difficulty in understanding how to proceed with a question or if your answer is incorrect and you are unable to identify why, that you ask for help from the teaching staff of your institution or consult textbooks or GCSE revision guides.

Links to the Minimum Core:

The Minimum Core lists the following knowledge and skills for algebra:
- **working with unknown values and variables.**

The importance of this topic may be inferred from the following examples of use in professional life and application in subject areas:

Concept	Examples
Working with unknown values and variables	• Formulas in different contexts • Understand and use relevant formulae
Looking for and examining patterns	• Predicting the next number(s) in a series or sequence

Implicit throughout is the ability to check both calculations, using for example, inverse operations, and the reasonableness of any answers using rounding, estimating and checking.

Further examples of how you would use these skills in professional life and application in subject areas include:

- **the checking of spreadsheet calculations;**
- **understanding the concept of inverse operations.**

HINTS AND TIPS

Remember:

- brackets should be worked out first;
- then work out multiplications and divisions;
- finally work out additions and subtractions;
- take care over units – make sure you are using consistent units.

EXAMPLE

Skills audit Question 21

A lecturer is checking on the current, in amps, of a new cooling fan for her classroom.
The fan has a power rating of 2100 watts. The voltage of the electrical supply is 240 volts.
Use the formula

Power (in watts) = voltage (in volts) × current (in amps)

to find the current, in amps, through the fan.
Give your answer to the nearest whole number.
Solution:
(i)   The formula is

Power (in watts) = voltage (in volts) × current (in amps)

(ii)   substitute the values given so the formula now reads:
2100 = 240 × C where C is the current.
(iii)   to find C divide 2100 by 240 giving
C = 8.75 amps
To the nearest whole number this is 9 amps

Key information

- You need to know the order in which to perform operations – basically multiply and divide before you add and subtract.
- You need to know and be able to use the commutative, associative and distributive rules – see Question 10.
- When algebraic formulas are written, 10b means $10 \times b$ and $\frac{10}{b}$ means $10 \div b$.

Key questions

Q1 Travel and Tourism students were given the following question to answer:

> **Fair Deal Car Hire**
>
> **£115 per day**
>
> **80 free miles for each day hired**
>
> **Extra distance charged at 60p per mile**

(a) Tom hires a car for 1 day and travels 250 miles.
How much does this cost?

(b) Amy hires a car for 5 days and drives 350 miles.
How much does this cost her?

(c) Imran hires a car for p days and drives q miles. Assuming that Imran drives more than 80 miles per day find an expression for the cost in terms of p and q.

Q2 To change a speed in metres per second into speed in miles per hour the formula is:

$$v = \frac{11}{5} \times s$$

where v is speed in miles per hour and s is speed in metres per second.

(a) An athlete can run at 10 metres per second.
What speed is this in miles per hour?

(b) Drag cars reach speeds of 100 miles per hour.
What speed is this in metres per second?

Q3 The following figure shows the outline of a pond:

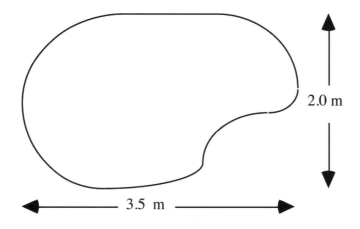

2.0 m

3.5 m

The maximum depth of the pond will be 0.9 metres.

The pond will need lining with a rectangular sheet of butyl. The size of sheet required is given by the following formula:

Length of pond liner = maximum length of pond + (2 × maximum depth) + 1.5
Width of pond liner = maximum width of pond + (2 × maximum depth) + 1.5

Calculate the size of pond liner needed.

Q4 Jamie says, 'I think of a whole number. I multiply it by 3 and add 5. The answer is a prime number between 20 and 30'.

Which of the following would you need to solve to find the number Jamie thought of?

(a) $3(n + 5) = 23$
(b) $3(n + 5) = 29$
(c) $3n + 5 = 23$
(d) $3n + 5 = 29$

What was the number Jamie thought of?

Q5 A printer calculates the cost of leaflets for a summer fair at a college using the formula:

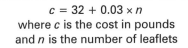

$$c = 32 + 0.03 \times n$$
where c is the cost in pounds
and n is the number of leaflets

How much does it cost to print 500 leaflets?

Q6 The power rating of electrical equipment is measured in watts.
It is calculated from the formula $P = VI$ where P is the power in watts,
V is the voltage rating and I is the current in amps.
Use the formula to find:

(a) P when $V = 220$ volts and $I = 10$ amps.

(b) I when $V = 220$ volts and $P = 880$ watts.

Q7 The total resistance of two electrical components connected together is given by the formula:

$$\text{total resistance} = \frac{Rr}{R + r}$$

If $R = 20$ and $r = 5$

calculate the total resistance.

Q8 Here is part of a spreadsheet showing some of the formulas.

Work out the values of the numbers in the shaded cells.

	A	B	C	D
1	1	1	= A1*B1	= A1 + B1 + C1
2	= A 1 + 1	= B 1 + 3	= A2*B2	= A2 + B2 + C2
3	= A 2 + 1	= B 2 + 3	= A3*B3	= A3 + B3 + C3
4	= A 3 + 1	= B 3 + 3	40	= A4*B4 + C4
5	5	13	65	= A5 + B5 + C5
6	6	16	96	118
7	7	19	133	159
8	8	22	176	206

Q9 Here are two formulas for converting temperature between Celsius (°C) and Fahrenheit (°F).

(a) F = 1.8C + 32

    (i)   use this formula to calculate the temperature in Fahrenheit when C = 15°

    (ii) use this formula to calculate the temperature in Celsius when F = 50°

    (iii) use this formula to calculate the temperature in Celsius when F = 100°

(b) F = (C + 40) × $\frac{9}{5}$ − 40

    (i)   use this formula to calculate the temperature in Fahrenheit when C = 25°

    (ii) use this formula to calculate the temperature in Celsius when F = 140°

    (iii) use this formula to calculate the temperature in Celsius when F = −40°

Q10 In the following table write whether the statements are true or false. Where you have indicated a statement is true, write whether it is a statement of the commutative, associative or distributive law.

	True/false	Which law?
$a + b = b + a$		
$(a + b) + c = a + (b + c)$		
$a \times b = b \times a$		
$a - b = b - a$		
$(a - b) - c = a - (b - c)$		
$a \times (b + c) = a \times b + b \times c$		
$(a \div b) \div c = a \div (b \div c)$		
$(a - b) \times c = a \times c - b \times c$		
$(a \times b) \times c = a \times (b \times c)$		

Q11 A civil engineering student uses the following formula:

$$w = \frac{h}{4} + 12$$

to calculate the dimensions of a trench to be dug out for a pipe to be laid.

The following diagram shows the cross-section of the trench:

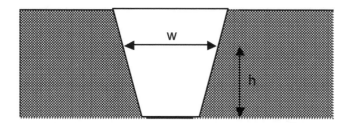

(i)   Find *w* when *h* = 10.

(ii) Find *h* when *w* = 17.

(iii) find *h* when *w* = 13.5.

Q12 To find the time needed to cook a piece of beef multiply the weight of the beef, in kilo-grams by 40 and add 10.

How many minutes are needed to cook a piece of beef weighing 3 kilograms?

Q13 This formula tells you the number of heaters needed to heat an office.

$$\text{number of heaters} = \frac{\text{length of office} \times \text{width of office}}{10}$$

An office measures 18 m by 12 m.

How many heaters are needed?

Q14 A student gained the following marks in tests A, B and C

Test	A	B	C
Raw mark	68	28	5

The student's weighted score is calculated using the following formula:

$$\text{weighted score} = \frac{(A \times 60)}{100} + \frac{(B \times 30)}{100} + C$$

Calculate the student's weighted score. Give your answer to the nearest whole number.

Q15 A sequence of numbers starts at 11 and follows the rule:

Double the last number and subtract 3

11   19   35   67   131   ....

The number 4099 is in this sequence.

Calculate the number which comes immediately before 4099 in the sequence.

Q16 The following number sequence follows the rule:

Double the last number and subtract 3

Which two numbers are missing?

....   120   11   0.1   ....

Q17 Here are the first four numbers in a number sequence:

10   13   16   8   ....

To get the next number in the sequence the rule is:

Look at the last number. If it is a multiple of 4, divide by 2. If it is not a multiple of 4 then add 3.

(a) What are the next five numbers in the sequence?

(b) Work out the 500th number in the sequence and show how you determined what it is.

(c) This sequence of numbers follows the same rule.

.... 14   17   20   10   13

The first three numbers are missing.
What could these three numbers be?

Q18 This diagram shows a number pattern made from triangles:

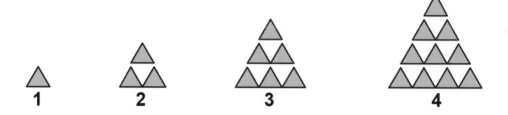

(a) Write down an expression in terms of *n* which represents this number pattern.

(b) Calculate the number of triangles in the 20th pattern.

Q19 Look at this sequence of circles. The first four patterns in the sequence have been drawn:

How many circles are there in the 100th pattern?

Q20 A theatre agency charges £25 per ticket, plus an overall booking charge of £3.

(a) Copy and complete the table.

Number of tickets	1	2	3	4
Cost in £				

(b) Write an expression for the cost, in pounds, of *n* tickets.

(c) Jenna pays £128 for her tickets. How many does she buy?

A SUMMARY OF KEY POINTS

In this chapter you have learnt how to:

> **use appropriate reasoning, strategies and techniques to solve problems;**

> **apply appropriate knowledge of algebra and skills in algebra;**

> **substitute numbers into formulas;**

> **solve simple equations.**

REFERENCES AND FURTHER READING REFERENCES AND FURTHER READING

There are few books specifically targeted at algebra. Most GCSE textbooks written for the higher tier of entry will cover the algebra content.

However, some useful sources of further reading at an appropriate level are:

Cooke, H., Houssart, J. and Mason, J. (2001) *Passport to Numeracy*. Buckingham: Open University Press.

Mooney, C., Ferrie, L., Fox, S., Hansen, A. and Wrathmell, R. (2009) *Primary Mathematics: Knowledge and Understanding* (4th ed.). Exeter: Learning Matters.

Websites

www.nrich.maths.org.uk
www.cimt.plymouth.ac.uk
www.bbc.co.uk/gcsebitesize
www.bbc.co.uk/revision

5
Shape and space

By the end of this chapter you should be able to:

- use appropriate methods, operations and tools to explore a situation and solve problems;
- use appropriate reasoning, strategies and techniques to solve problems;
- apply appropriate knowledge of shapes and skills in shape;
- assess your own level of understanding in the context of shape.

This chapter and the objectives contribute to the following Minimum Core requirements: Part B: Personal Numeracy Skills: Processes.

This chapter also contributes to the following LLUK Standards:
AS4, AS7, AP4.2, BS2, CK1.1, CK1.2, CP1.1, CK3.4, CP3.4.

Introduction

This chapter provides you with an opportunity to check your understanding of the knowledge and skills in shape and space. The Minimum Core also states that you should be able to use knowledge of related problems and in this chapter there are clear, but implicit links to the number content. The Minimum Core sets out that personal skills in numeracy, (here shape and space), include, amongst other things, *the ability to communicate about numeracy concepts, to develop one's own understanding of numeracy concepts and recognise and analyse misconceptions, (and misunderstandings).* The range of topics here includes 2D and 3D shapes. The contents of this chapter are intended to cover the list given below in the 'Links to the Minimum Core'. It is important that if you do have difficulty in understanding how to proceed with a question or if your answer is incorrect and you are unable to identify why, that you ask for help from the teaching staff of your institution or consult textbooks or GCSE revision guides.

Links to the Minimum Core:

The Minimum Core lists the following knowledge and skills for shape and space:
- **having a knowledge of and using the properties of common 2D and 3D shapes;**
- **creating and interpreting 2D representations of 3D objects.**

The importance of these topics may be inferred from the following examples of use in professional life and application in subject areas:

Concept	Examples
Having a knowledge of and using the properties of common 2D and 3D shapes	• Organising teaching space • Use of the correct language for 2D and 3D shapes
Creating and interpreting 2D representations of 3D objects	• Designing kitchens

Implicit throughout is the ability to check both calculations, using for example, inverse operations, and the reasonableness of any answers using rounding, estimating and checking. Further examples of how you would use these skills in professional life and application in subject areas include:
• **best layout of workspace;**
• **garden design;**
• **efficient storage and packaging;**
• **use of scales, comparing scales;**
• **use of non-rectangular work surfaces.**

HINTS AND TIPS
• If you want to find the area of a complex shape, split it up into simpler shapes (rectangles, triangles, circles) and find the required area by adding or subtracting the areas of these simpler shapes.
• Make sure that measurements are in the same units before using them in calculations.
• When you want to find missing angles, see if you can identify angles that must be equal or that must add up to 180° or 360°.
• Always sketch diagrams if they are not provided.

EXAMPLE
For the shape opposite, draw
(a) the plan;
(b) the front elevation (view from F);
(c) the side elevation from S.

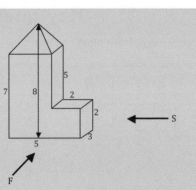

Solution:
(a) Plan

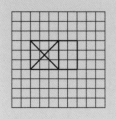

The cross shows the edges of the pyramid on top of the tower. The rectangle on the right is the flat top of the lower part of the shape.

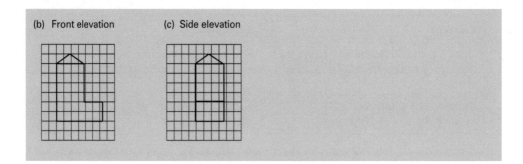

(b) Front elevation   (c) Side elevation

Key information

- Angles in a triangle add up to 180°.
- Angles in a quadrilateral add up to 360°.

 These are opposite angles and are equal.

 These are alternate angles and are equal.

 These are complementary angles and add up to 180°.

These are corresponding angles and are equal.

- Triangles that are congruent are exactly the same.
- Triangles that are similar have the same shape, ie the angles are the same, but they may be of different sizes.

Key questions

Q1 Here is a shape made from plastic cubes:

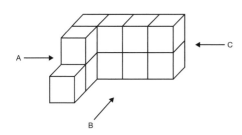

(a) How many cubes have been used?

(b) Three views of the shape are shown below.

Write underneath each view whether it is seen from A or from B or from C.

        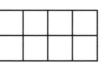

(i) ....   (ii) ....   (iii) ....

Q2 (a) On the grid below draw a triangle with one right angle.

(b) On the grid below draw a quadrilateral with only two right angles.

(c) On the grid below draw a pentagon with only three right angles.

Q3 Here are some shapes made out of centimetre squares:

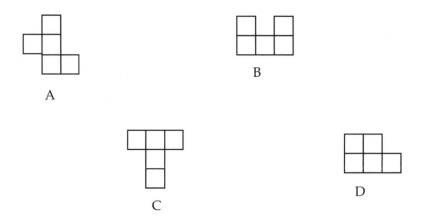

(a) Which ones will not fold up to make an open box?

(b) Which one does not have a perimeter of 12cm?

Q4 Sketch the plan view, front elevation and side elevations of these objects:

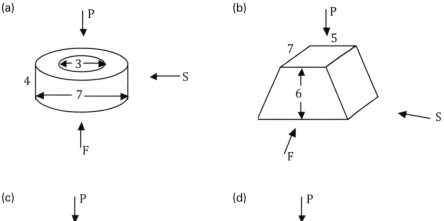

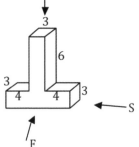

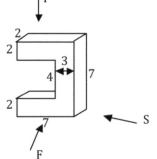

Q5

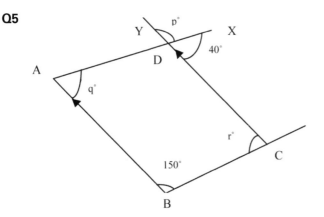

In the diagram AX and CY are straight lines that intersect at D.

BA and CY are parallel.

Angle CDX = 40° and angle ABC = 150°.

Find the size of angles p, q and r.

Q6 Find angles a and b giving your reasons.

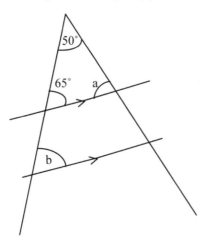

Q7 What is the size of angle a and angle b?

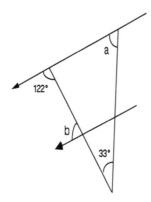

Q8 Copy and complete this table showing the properties that are always true for the special quadrilaterals:

	Sides		Diagonals	Parallel sides	
Quadrilateral	Four equal sides	Two different pairs of equal sides	Equal diagonals	Two pairs of parallel sides	Only one pair of parallel sides
Square	✓		✓	✓	
Rectangle		✓	✓	✓	
Rhombus					
Parallelogram					
Trapezium					
Kite					

Q9 Calculate the third angle in each of these triangles.

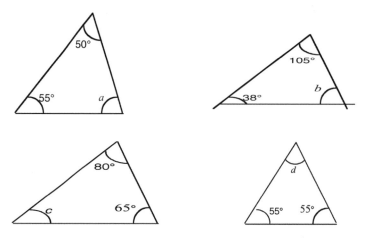

Q10 PQR is a triangle. Angle QPR = 58° and angle PQR = 65°.

Sketch the triangle and find angle PRQ.

Q11 PQR is a triangle. PRS is a straight line. Angle QPR = 48° and angle PQR = 63°.

Calculate angle x.

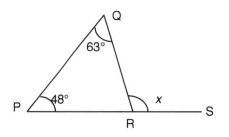

Q12 ABCD is a rectangle.

P is halfway between B and C.

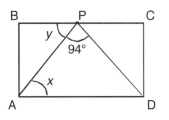

(a) What type of triangle is APD?

(b) Calculate the angles x and y.

Q13 (a) Which of these triangles is congruent to triangle A?

(b) Which of these triangles is similar to triangle A?

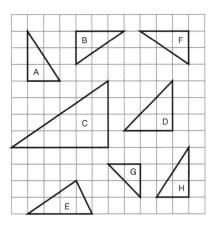

Q14 A box has edges 5 cm, 6 cm and 3 cm.

Is it a cube or a cuboid? Explain your answer.

Q15 Draw a net of this closed box.

Label the lengths of each edge.

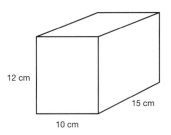

12 cm

15 cm

10 cm

A SUMMARY OF KEY POINTS

In this chapter you have learnt how to:

> **use appropriate methods, operations and tools to explore a situation and solve problems;**

> **use appropriate reasoning, strategies and techniques to solve problems;**

> **apply appropriate knowledge of shapes and skills in shape;**

> **sketch and interpret drawings and draw or sketch nets of objects.**

REFERENCES AND FURTHER READING REFERENCES AND FURTHER READING

There are few books specifically targeted at shape and space. Most GCSE textbooks written for the higher tier of entry will cover the shape and space content.

However, some useful sources of further reading at an appropriate level are:

Cooke, H., Houssart, J. and Mason, J. (2001) *Passport to Numeracy*. Buckingham: Open University Press.

Mooney, C., Ferrie, L., Fox, S., Hansen, A. and Wrathmell, R. (2009) *Primary Mathematics: Knowledge and Understanding*. (4th ed.) Exeter: Learning Matters.

Websites

www.nrich.maths.org.uk
www.cimt.plymouth.ac.uk
www.bbc.co.uk/gcsebitesize
www.bbc.co.uk/revision

6
Measures

By the end of this chapter you should be able to:

- use appropriate methods, operations and tools to explore a situation and solve problems;
- use appropriate reasoning, strategies and techniques to solve problems;
- apply appropriate knowledge of measures and skills in measures;
- assess your own level of understanding in the context of measurement.

This chapter and the objectives contribute to the following Minimum Core requirements:
Part B: Personal Numeracy Skills: Processes.

This chapter also contributes to the following LLUK Standards:
AS4, AS7, AP4.2, BS2, CK1.1, CK1.2, CP1.1, CK3.4, CP3.4.

Introduction

This chapter provides you with an opportunity to check your understanding of the knowledge and skills in measures. The Minimum Core also states that you should be able to use knowledge of related problems and in this chapter there are clear, but implicit links to the number content. The Minimum Core sets out that personal skills in numeracy, (here measures), include, amongst other things, *the ability to communicate about numeracy concepts, to develop one's own understanding of numeracy concepts and recognise and analyse misconceptions, (and misunderstandings).* The range of topics here is quite extensive. It is essential that you are familiar with the common metric units and how to convert between, for example, kilometres and millimetres and also be able to work with the common, (everyday) imperial units and with conversion charts and tables. The contents of this chapter are intended to cover the list given below in the 'Links to the Minimum Core'. It is important that if you do have difficulty in understanding how to proceed with a question or if your answer is incorrect and you are unable to identify why, that you ask for help from the teaching staff of your institution or consult textbooks or GCSE revision guides.

Links to the Minimum Core:

The Minimum Core lists the following knowledge and skills for measures:
- **working with area, perimeter, volume and capacity of shapes;**
- **interpreting and using rates of change;**
- **working with money, metric and where appropriate imperial units;**
- **using conversion tables and scales.**

The importance of these topics may be inferred from the following examples of use in professional life and application in subject areas:

Concept	Examples
Working with area, perimeter, volume and capacity of shapes	• Organising teaching space • Organising display space • Designing a kitchen
Interpreting and using rates of change	• Understanding how to solve problems involving change of angle
Working with money, metric and where appropriate imperial units	• Costs of items, best value, comparisons of costs
Using conversion tables and scales	• Converting between temperatures • Converting between metric and imperial

Implicit throughout is the ability to check both calculations, using for example, inverse operations, and the reasonableness of any answers using rounding, estimating and checking.

Further examples of how you would use these skills in professional life and application in subject areas include:
- **meeting health and safety requirements;**
- **understanding plans and elevations in technical drawings;**
- **design of publicity materials, eg the effect of dimensional change;**
- **comparison of maps with different scales.**

HINTS AND TIPS
- If you want to find the area of a complex shape, split it up into simpler shapes (rectangles, triangles, circles) and find the required area by adding or subtracting the areas of these simpler shapes.
- Make sure that measurements are in the same units before using them in calculations.

EXAMPLE
Skills audit Question 1
This is a drawing of a classroom wall.
The shaded area will be used as a noticeboard.
What is the shaded area?

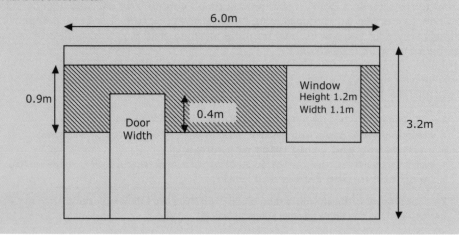

Solution:
The shaded area without window, part of door = 6 x 0.9 = 5.4m².
The window area = 0.9 x 1.1 = 0.994m².
The area of the door overlapping the shaded area = 0.4 x 0.9 = 0.36m².
Therefore shaded area required = 5.4 – 0.99 – 0.36 = 4.05m².

Key information

The area of a circle is given by πr^2, the circumference is $2\pi r$ or πd, where r is the radius and d is the diameter of the circle.

You should know the following:

Length: 1 kilometre = 1000 metres.
            1 metre = 100 centimetres or 1000 millimetres.
            1 centimetre = 10 millimetres.
Mass: 1 kilogram = 1000 grams.
            1 tonne = 1000 kilograms.
Capacity: 1 litre = 1000 millilitres = 100 centilitres.

And that distance = speed × time.

Key questions

Q1 The layout of a classroom is shown below. There are 30 grey tables. Each table is square with a side length of 50cm.

The grey tables are moved to the side of the room.

The rest of the room can be used for practical work.

What is the ratio of the practical area to the area covered by tables? Write your answer in its simplest form.

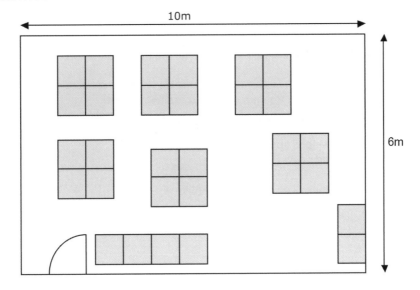

Q2 Which of these is the longest measurement?

85cm   2km   150mm   20m

Q3 Percy is a student on a Horticulture course. He can use a heated greenhouse in winter to grow summer bedding plants.

The temperature in the greenhouse has to be kept at a constant 15°C.

(a) If the temperature outside is –7°C what is the difference between this temperature and the temperature in the greenhouse?

Percy will arrange the bedding plants round the edge of a circular flower bed in the college grounds. The flower bed has a radius of 5m. The plants have to be set 25 cm apart.

(b) About how many plants will he need?

Q4 While on a cycle ride, a cyclist notices that her bicycle's front wheel is rotating exactly three times every second. The diameter of the wheel is 0.71 metres.

Use the formula circumference = π × diameter, where π = 3.142 to find the speed of her bicycle in metres per second, to the nearest tenth.

Q5 The following diagram shows a sketch of a sandpit to be built in a college nursery's ground.

The sandpit will be circular in shape, 3.5 metres in diameter and will be 0.6 metres deep.

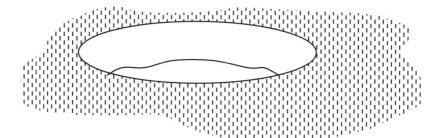

(a) Calculate the volume of sand required to fill the pit up to the top.

Use the formula:

$$\text{Volume} = 3.142 \times \text{radius}^2 \times \text{depth.}$$

(b) Use the following information to estimate the cost of the sand:

- 1m³ of sand weighs about 1.8 tonnes;
- 1 tonne of sand costs £15.

Q6 The area of a trapezium is given by the formula:

$$\frac{1}{2}(a + b) \times h$$

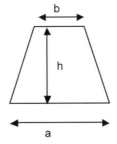

Calculate the area of the trapezium if a = 4 cm, b = 3 cm and h = 6 cm.

Q7 Some students on a Construction course were asked to calculate the volume of concrete needed to make these garden steps. All three steps are the same size.

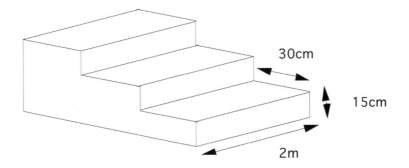

Calculate the volume of the steps.

Q8 The following diagram shows a circle and a square.

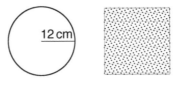

(a) The radius of the circle is 12 cm.

What is the circumference of the circle?

take $\pi = 3$

(b) The ratio of the circumference of the circle to the perimeter of the square is 1 : 2.

(i) What is the perimeter of the square?

(ii) What is the length of a side of the square?

(c) A triangle is drawn that just fits inside the square.

What is the area of the triangle?

Q9 A careers lecturer makes some circular name tags from sheets of card. The circular tags are 60 mm in diameter.

The sheets of card measure 20 centimetres by 30 centimetres.

What is the maximum number of name tags she can cut from each card?

Q10 A college is to have a new theatre.

The following plan below shows the intended seating area:

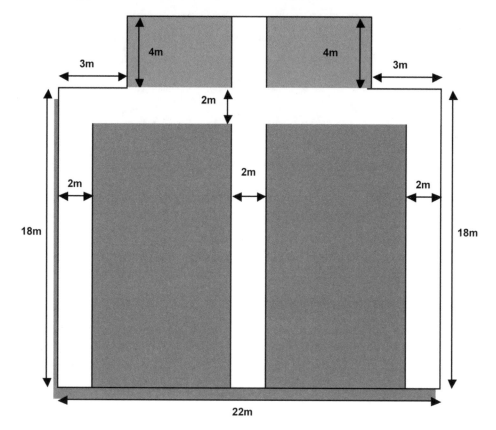

The shaded area will have seats. Each seat will take up a space 1 m × 1 m.

(a) How many seats will fit into the seating area?

An architect is to make a scale model of the theatre. The scale he uses is 1:50.

(b) What will be the width of the model?

Q11 A college is building a garden for staff and students to sit in. The focal point of the garden will be a circular pond, 4.5 metres in diameter. For safety reasons the pond will have a small fence around it 0.5 metres from the edge.

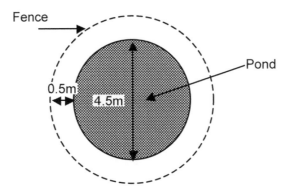

(a) Using the formula

Circumference = $2\pi r$ calculate the length of fence needed. Take $\pi = 3.1$.

(b) The fence is to be 0.2m high. What is the area of the fence?

Both sides of the fence are to be treated with green wood preservative. Preservative is sold in 2-litre tins which cost £15.00. One litre of preservative will cover 6 m².

(c) How much will it cost to treat the fence?

Q12 The distance around the grounds of a college is measured as $3\frac{1}{2}$ miles.

(a) Using the fact that 5 miles = 8 kilometres, how far is this in kilometres?

(b) A lecturer decides to walk round the grounds each day in order to keep fit. If he walks at 4 miles per hour how long will it take him to cover the distance?

Q13 Using the relationships:

1 foot = 12 inches and 1 metre is approximately 39 inches.

Change 60 feet into metres.

Q14 A scale drawing of a room has a length of 210mm and a width of 130mm. If the scale is 1:40 what are the length and width of the room in metres.

Q15 A course is to be delivered in two-hour sessions on Mondays and Wednesdays. The tutor has been allocated 60 hours of contact time. The course will begin on Monday 3 September. Use the following calendar to work out when it will finish. Holidays and weekends are shaded out.

	September						October				
M		3	10	17	24	M	1	8	15	22	29
T		4	11	18	25	T	2	9	16	23	30
W		5	12	19	26	W	3	10	17	24	31
T		6	13	20	27	T	4	11	18	25	
F		7	14	21	28	F	5	12	19	26	
S	1	8	15	22	29	S	6	13	20	27	
S	2	9	16	23	30	S	7	14	21	28	

	November						December				
M		5	12	19	26	M		3	10	17	24
T		6	13	20	27	T		4	11	18	25
W		7	14	21	28	W		5	12	19	26
T	1	8	15	22	29	T		6	13	20	27
F	2	9	16	23	30	F		7	14	21	28
S	3	10	17	24		S	1	8	15	22	29
S	4	11	18	25		S	2	9	16	23	30

Q16 (a) The distance from a college to a ferry port is 135 miles.

The average speed for a coach for the journey, allowing for stops and delays, is 40 miles per hour.

What is the expected length of the journey, to the nearest half-hour?

(b) The ferry will sail at 17.00 hours and boarding must be completed 45 minutes before this.

What is the latest time to leave the college in order to be at the port in time? Give your answer in 24-hour clock time.

Q17 The following is part of a chart showing the distance in miles between some places in England.

	Birmingham	Bristol	Carlisle	Dover	Exeter	Hull	Leeds	Lincoln	Liverpool	London	Manchester
Birmingham											
Bristol	80										
Carlisle	199	282									
Dover	207	206	400								
Exeter	164	84	355	244							
Hull	134	231	170	264	305						
Leeds	116	212	126	271	286	60					
Lincoln	99	186	182	220	260	47	72				
Liverpool	102	184	126	304	258	128	74	140			
London	120	120	313	72	200	187	198	143	215		
Manchester	89	172	123	291	291	97	44	85	35	202	
Nottingham	52	145	188	218	218	92	74	38	112	131	71

Rob is a salesman. Use the chart to work out how far he travels if his journey is from Bristol to Liverpool to Leeds to Nottingham to Bristol.

Q18 A family of four is planning to use the 'Skylink' shuttle bus from Nottingham city centre to the airport to catch their holiday flight. The flight is scheduled to take off at 17.30. They have to have completed their check-in an hour before take-off and they reckon the family will take 10 minutes to check in. They also allow for the check-in queue to take an hour and a half.

The bus leaves the city centre every 30 minutes – journey time is approximately 45 minutes to the Arrivals terminal. The first bus leaves the city centre at 04:05. Allow 5 minutes or so to walk from the Arrivals to the Departures hall.

What is the departure time of the last bus that they should aim to catch to enable them to be on their flight?

Q19 The construction department at a college store building materials in a metal skip. The dimensions of the skip are shown in the following diagram:

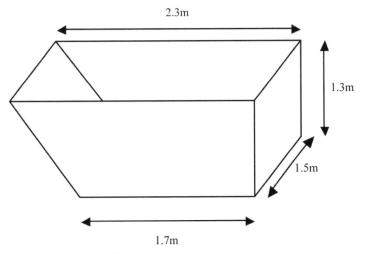

The sides of the skip are in the form of a trapezium.

You will need to know the following formulas:

The area of a trapezium = $\frac{1}{2}$ (the sum of the parallel sides) × perpendicular distance between them.

The volume of a shape like this skip = cross-sectional area × depth.

Calculate the volume of the skip.

A SUMMARY OF KEY POINTS

In this chapter you have learnt how to:

> use appropriate methods, operations and tools to explore a situation and solve problems;

> use appropriate reasoning, strategies and techniques to solve problems;

> apply appropriate knowledge of measures and skills in measures;

> calculate lengths, areas and volumes of simple and compound shapes.

REFERENCES AND FURTHER READING REFERENCES AND FURTHER READING

There are few books specifically targeted at measures. Most GCSE textbooks written for the higher tier of entry will cover the measures content.

However, some useful sources of further reading at an appropriate level are:

Cooke, H., Houssart, J. and Mason, J. (2001) *Passport to Numeracy*. Buckingham: Open University Press.

Mooney, C., Ferrie, L., Fox, S., Hansen, A. and Wrathmell, R. (2009) *Primary Mathematics: Knowledge and Understanding*. (4th ed.) Exeter: Learning Matters.

Websites

www.nrich.maths.org.uk
www.cimt.plymouth.ac.uk
www.bbc.co.uk/gcsebitesize
www.bbc.co.uk/revision

7
Handling data

By the end of this chapter you should be able to:

- use appropriate methods, operations and tools to explore a situation and solve problems;
- use appropriate reasoning, strategies and techniques to solve problems;
- apply appropriate knowledge of data and skills in handling data;
- assess your own level of understanding in the context of data;
- make sense of data.

This chapter and the objectives contribute to the following Minimum Core requirements:
Part B: Personal Numeracy Skills: Processes.

This chapter also contributes to the following LLUK Standards:
AS4, AS7, AP4.2, BS2, CK1.1, CK1.2, CP1.1, CK3.4, CP3.4.

Introduction

This chapter provides you with an opportunity to check your understanding of the data handling knowledge and skills, which implicitly include using diagrams, charts and graphs. You need to understand the difference between discrete and continuous data and how to draw and interpret the statistical diagrams that often appear in, for example, Ofsted reports. The Minimum Core also states that you should be able to use knowledge of related problems and in this chapter there are clear, but implicit links to the number content. The Minimum Core sets out that personal skills in numeracy, (here data handling), include, amongst other things, *the ability to communicate about numeracy concepts, to develop one's own understanding of numeracy concepts and recognise and analyse misconceptions, (and misunderstandings).* The contents of this chapter are intended to cover the list given below in the 'Links to the Minimum Core'. It is important that if you do have difficulty in understanding how to proceed with a question or if your answer is incorrect and you are unable to identify why, that you ask for help from the teaching staff of your institution or consult textbooks or GCSE revision guides.

Links to the Minimum Core:

The Minimum Core lists the following knowledge and skills for handling data:
- **manipulating discrete and continuous data;**
- **understanding and creating frequency diagrams, pie charts and scatter diagrams.**

The importance of these topics may be inferred from the following examples of use in professional life and application in subject areas:

Concept	Examples
Manipulating discrete and continuous data	• Extracting information from diagrams, tables and graphs
Understanding and creating frequency diagrams, pie charts and scatter diagrams	• Trends in course achievement, attendance and gender/age balance • Understanding the key ideas of regression and correlation

Implicit throughout is the ability to check both calculations, using for example, inverse operations, and the reasonableness of any answers using rounding, estimating and checking. Further examples of how you would use these skills in professional life and application in subject areas include:
- **interpretation of customer/lifestyle surveys;**
- **analysis of modes of transport to and from workplace/college;**
- **interpretation of inspection findings or value added data;**
- **using Body Mass Index;**
- **health issues such as the link between smoking and heart problems;**
- **students' perception of courses;**
- **interpretation of inspection findings.**

HINTS AND TIPS
- The mean, median and mode are all types of average and they give an idea of the 'middle' or the expected value of a data set. The range measures how widely spread the data are.
- If you are asked to compare two or more data sets, comment on differences or similarities in both the average you are using and the range.
- When working with grouped data you do not know exactly what values the data had so if you need to estimate the mean or range of grouped data you should assume that all the measurements that fall within a particular interval are at the midpoint of that interval.
- When choosing a sample, make sure that every individual in the group you are sampling from has an equal chance of being selected. This will ensure that your sample is random.
- Cumulative frequency represents a running total and each point on the cumulative frequency curve gives the number (or %) of values which are less than the corresponding value on the horizontal axis. A cumulative frequency graph is often used to answer a question such as, 'what percentage of students gained a pass mark of 55 on a test?'.

EXAMPLES

Example 1
Skills audit Question 12

A survey of leisure time and part-time work of students in a college is to be carried out. The sample size is to be approximately one-third of the student population.

Which of the following methods would provide an appropriate sample?
(a) Pick from the registers those born on the 3rd, 6th, 9th etc. of each month.
(b) Pick every third student in the cafeteria.
(c) Ask for volunteers and pick one-third of them.
(d) Obtain an alphabetical list of all students and pick every third name.

Solution:

The answer is (d).

(a), (b) and (c) would give biased samples and (b) and (c) would not address the need to sample from the whole student population.

Example 2

A survey of leisure time and part-time work of students in a college has been conducted. The mean values of the responses are recorded on the following form.

Activity	Mean hours spent per week	
	Males	**Females**
Computer/Internet	6.5	3.5
Shopping	2.5	6
Socialising	4	7.5
Sport/exercise	3	1.5
TV	7	9
Paid work	7	5

Based on the values in this table, state whether you agree with the following statements, giving your reasons:

(i)   Most women spend 1.5 hours a week doing sport/exercising.

(ii)   Some men spend 4 hours a week socialising.

(iii)   On average, men spend 3 hours a week longer on computers than women do.

(iv)   Nobody does more than 7 hours paid work per week.

(v)   The overall mean number of hours spent watching TV for males and females together is 8.

Solution:

(i)   No. The values in the table are mean values and tell us nothing about individual responses or the distribution of the data so this is not necessarily true.

(ii)   No. It is possible that no male socialised for 4 hours: the mean of 1, 3, 5 and 7 is 4 but none of the individual values are 4 so it is possible to obtain a mean of 4 without any of the values being 4.

(iii)   Yes. The mean is an average and the mean for males is 3 hours more than the mean for females so this is true.

(iv)   No. 7 is the mean value, not the maximum value, so this is unlikely to be true. It could only be true if all males had given 7 hours as their response.

(v)   No. We would need to calculate a weighted mean based on the numbers of males and females surveyed but we do not have this information.

Key information

- The mean is found by adding up all the values in a list and dividing the total by the number of values.
- The median is the middle value when all the values in a list have been put in order.
- The mode is the most common value.
- The range is the difference between the highest value and the lowest value.

Key questions

Q1 Which of the following measures would show the difference between the maximum and minimum temperatures?

Mean   Median   Mode   Range

Q2 The responses to the 'paid work' question (see Audit Question 13), for one group of students were:

Female	11	12	9	7	8.5	11.5	2	8		
Male	9	10.5	3	6	12.5	0	9	11	6	12

What are the mean times worked per week for females and for males (to the nearest half-hour)?

Q3 A group of A level students is investigating what width-to-height proportions in abstract shapes are the most pleasing to people. They show a sliding rectangle (as below) to people stopped at random in the street, adjusting the rectangle in and out and asking each person to say when they feel the proportions of the rectangle are the most satisfying. The rectangle is fixed at 10 cm high and can be adjusted so that it is anywhere between 10 and 20 cm wide.

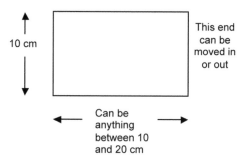

10 cm

This end can be moved in or out

Can be anything between 10 and 20 cm

Their first 20 results (in centimetres) are:

15.5	16.6	17.4	16.1	17.7	15.2	17.5
18.3	19.1	16.4	17.5	13.8	16.4	16.6
17.2	16.8	16.9	18.3	14.5	15.3	

(a) Complete the following table showing their results:

Width measurement in cm	Frequency F	Midpoint X	F x X
13.00–13.99		13.5	
14.00–14.99		14.5	
15.00–15.99			
16.00–16.99			
17.00–17.99			
18.00–18.99		18.5	
19.00–19.99		19.5	
Total			

(b) Use the table to estimate the mean width chosen.

(c) Calculate the mean width-to-height ratio.

Q4 The percentage population in higher education between the years 1999 and 2002 in England, Scotland, Northern Ireland and Wales is shown by this bar chart:

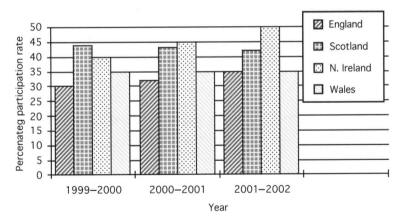

(a) Which country's participation rate decreased from 1999 to 2002?

(b) Which country's participation rate remained constant during this period?

(c) Which country's participation rate increased by the greatest amount over this period?

Q5 A French lecturer plotted this graph to compare the results of a French oral test and a French written test given to a group of 20 students.

The pass mark on each test was 55%.

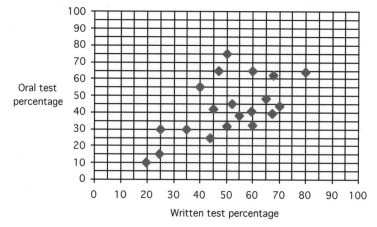

Which of the following statements is true?

(a) The range of marks for the oral test is greater than for the written test.

(b) A quarter of students achieved a higher mark on the oral test than on the written test.

(c) 20% of the pupils passed both tests.

Q6 The typical diet of a sportsman is given in the following table:

Food type	%	Angle
Carbohydrate	60	216°
Fat	25	
Protein	15	

(a) Calculate the angle of the sector which represents fat and complete the table.

(b) Draw the pie chart.

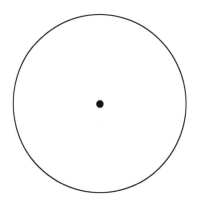

Q7 A lecturer produced this cumulative frequency graph to show the performance of students in his college in 2007 and 2008 who retook GCSE mathematics. There were 240 students in his analysis.

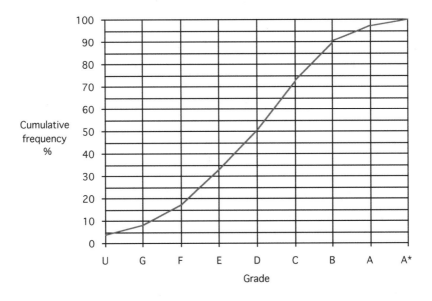

How many students gained a grade C or better?

Q8 There were 25 students in an A level history class.

One student was absent when there was an end-of-module test.

The mean test score for the class was 63.

On returning to college the absent student took the test and scored 93.

What was the revised mean test score for the whole class?

Give your answer correct to the nearest whole number.

Q9 A runner competes in nine half-marathons in one year.

This table shows her times:

1 hour 56 minutes
1 hour 48 minutes
2 hours 10 minutes
1 hour 56 minutes
1 hour 52 minutes
1 hour 59 minutes
2 hours 14 minutes
1 hour 45 minutes
1 hour 39 minutes

(a) What is the range of the times, in minutes?

(b) Calculate the mean time.

Q10 The manager of a cinema records the number of people attending the afternoon show-ing during one half-term week, from Monday to Friday.

Day of the week	Mon	Tues	Wed	Thurs	Frid
Number of adults	156	186	135	142	216
Number of children	44	89	52	62	98

(a) Calculate the mean number of adults who attended the afternoon show.

Tickets cost £6.50 for adults and £2.80 for children.

(b) Calculate how much money the cinema received from ticket sales for the afternoon show's on Monday and Tuesday.

Q11 A mature student works part time and earns £240 per week.

The following pie chart shows how she spends her wages:

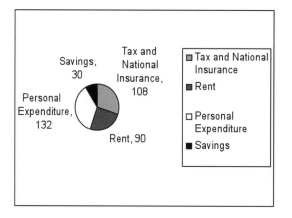

What fraction of her income does she manage to save each week?

Q12 A doctor surveys the ages of the patients at his morning surgery for three days. The table shows the results of his survey.

	Monday	Tuesday	Wednesday
Males	41, 76, 90, 19, 7	5, 25, 82, 45, 2, 53, 75, 52	52, 37, 4, 59, 82, 62
Females	63, 79, 21, 33, 24, 16, 71	45, 62, 73, 35, 22, 18, 3	83, 33, 94, 14, 88, 2

He uses the data to construct a frequency table:

	Under 20	20 to 39	40 to 60	Over 60
Males	5	2	6	6
Females	5	6	1	7

(a) There is a mistake in this frequency table. Which entry is wrong?

(b) What is the mean age of the females surveyed?

(c) What fraction of all those surveyed were aged between 40 and 60?

Q13 A golfer keeps a check of his scores each season. For 2008 his scores were:

Score	69	70	71	72	73	74	75	76	77	78	79
Frequency	2	2	4	2	3	3	2	2	2	1	2

(a) What was his median score?

(b) What percentage of his scores were less than 74?

(c) For 2009 he sets himself a target of having a mean score of 74. What is the percentage improvement he will have to make compared with the 2008 mean score?

Q14 A student takes five literacy tests and four numeracy tests.

The scores she achieves in each test are shown in the following table:

Test	1	2	3	4	5
Numeracy	61	59	64	72	
Literacy	59	68	63	62	63

(a) What is the difference in the mean scores for literacy and numeracy?

(b) She needs to achieve a mean score of 68 in numeracy. What mark must she gain in test 5 for numeracy in order to achieve this?

Q15 (Look back at the Example Question 2) The responses are recorded on the following form:

Activity	Mean number of hours spent per week (to the nearest half-hour)	
	Males	Females
Computer/Internet	6.5	3.5
Shopping	2.5	6
Socialising	4	7.5
Sport	3	1.5
TV	7	9
Paid work	7	5

Write down three comments which compare the activities of males and females.

(i)   ....

(ii)   ....

(iii) ....

A SUMMARY OF KEY POINTS

In this chapter you have learnt how to:

> **use appropriate methods, operations and tools to explore a situation and solve problems;**

> **use appropriate reasoning, strategies and techniques to solve problems;**

> **apply appropriate knowledge of data and skills in handling data;**

> **assess your own level of understanding in the context of data;**

> **make sense of data.**

REFERENCES AND FURTHER READING REFERENCES AND FURTHER READING

There are few books specifically targeted at data. Most GCSE textbooks written for the higher tier of entry will cover the data content.

However, some useful sources of further reading at an appropriate level are:

Cooke, H., Houssart, J. and Mason, J. (2001) *Passport to Numeracy*. Buckingham: Open University Press.

Mooney, C., Ferrie, L., Fox, S., Hansen, A. and Wrathmell, R. (2009) *Primary Mathematics: Knowledge and Understanding*. (4th ed.) Exeter: Learning Matters.

Websites
www.nrich.maths.org.uk
www.cimt.plymouth.ac.uk
www.bbc.co.uk/gcsebitesize
www.bbc.co.uk/revision

8
Probability

Introduction

This chapter provides you with an opportunity to check your understanding of the probability knowledge and skills, which implicitly include using tables and lists as well as the probability scale. The Minimum Core also states that you should be able to use knowledge of related problems and in this chapter there are clear, but implicit links to the number content. The Minimum Core sets out that personal skills in numeracy, (here probability),include, amongst other things, *the ability to communicate about numeracy concepts, to develop one's own understanding of numeracy concepts and recognise and analyse misconceptions, (and misunderstandings).* The contents of this chapter are intended to cover the list given below in the 'Links to the Minimum Core'. It is important that if you do have difficulty in understanding how to proceed with a question or if your answer is incorrect and you are unable to identify why, that you ask for help from the teaching staff of your institution or consult textbooks or GCSE revision guides.

Links to the Minimum Core:

The Minimum Core lists the following knowledge and skills for probability:
- **understanding likelihood or probability;**
- **using the probability scale from 0 to 1.**
The importance of these topics may be inferred from the following examples of use in professional life and application in subject areas:

Concept	Examples
Understanding likelihood or probability	• Evaluating the likelihood of courses running successfully
Using the probability scale from 0 to 1	• Calculating expected number of exam passes
Expressing probabilities as fractions, decimals or percentages	• Understanding survey findings

Implicit throughout is the ability to check both calculations, using for example, inverse operations, and the reasonableness of any answers using rounding, estimating and checking.

Further examples of how you would use these skills in professional life and application in subject areas include:

- **chance in planning events such as weather conditions for outdoor events;**
- **attendance;**
- **fund raising;**
- **using games.**

HINTS AND TIPS

- When you know in advance that all outcomes are equally likely, you can **calculate** probabilities. For example, if a fair 1–6 die is rolled the probability of getting a 4 is 1/6 (1 out of 6) because each outcome is equally likely and there are 6 possible outcomes, one of which is 4. The probability of getting an even number is 3/6 because there are 6 possible outcomes, three of which are even.
- Probabilities can also be estimated from data collected by observation, survey or experiment. In this case the probability of an outcome is given by its relative frequency, that is, the fraction of the total that outcome represents in the data.
- The probabilities of all possible outcomes must add up to 1 so, for example, if the probability of winning a game is 2/3 then the probability of not winning must be 1–2/3 = 1/3.
- If you know the probability of a particular outcome, the expected number of times that it will occur is given by probability × total number of events. So if you roll a fair die 240 times, you expect to get a four 1/6 × 240 = 40 times.

EXAMPLE

An analysis of test results over a three-year period shows that 136 students out of a total of 170 achieved the pass mark of 40%.

(a) What is the probability that a student chosen at random passed?

(b) What is the probability that a student chosen at random fails?

(c) If the probability of passing remains the same, how many students in a cohort of 50 would you expect to pass?

Solution:
(a) 136 out of 170 students passed so the probability that a student chosen at random passed can be expressed as the fraction 136/170, the number of students who passed divided by the total number of students. This can also be expressed as the decimal fraction 0.8 (136 ÷ 170).
(b) Remember that the probabilities of all possible outcomes (in this case, pass or fail) must add up to 1. So if the probability of passing is 0.8, the probability of failing is 1 – 0.8 = 0.2.
(c) The probability of passing can also be interpreted as the proportion of students who pass. So if 0.8 (or 136/170) is the proportion who pass, we expect 0.8 * 50 = 40 students to pass.

Key information

- Probabilities may be expressed as fractions or decimals between 0 and 1 or as percentages between 0 and 100. For example, the probability of getting a tail when a fair coin is thrown is ½ or 0.5 or 50% $= \dfrac{50}{100}$.
- An outcome that is certain has a probability of 1.
- An outcome that is impossible has a probability of 0.
- An outcome that is likely has a probability greater than 0.5.
- An outcome that is unlikely has a probability less than 0.5.

The probabilities for all possible outcomes must add up to 1. For example, when a fair coin is thrown p(head) + p(tail) $= \frac{1}{2} + \frac{1}{2} = 1$.

Key questions

Q1 The question, 'Do you undertake paid work for more than 16 hours a week?' was asked of 100 students. The results are shown in the following table:

	Yes	No	Total
Male	25	35	60
Female	12	28	40
Total	37	63	100

What is the probability that a randomly selected student

(a) is male?

(b) answered 'Yes'?

(c) answered 'Yes' and is female?

Q2 An exam paper comprises 30 multiple-choice questions, each of which has five possible answers to choose from.

(a) A candidate guesses the answer to question 20. What is the probability that they get the answer correct?

(b) Another candidate guesses the answers to all the questions. How many answers would you expect them to get correct out of 30?

(c) 100 candidates sit the exam and all of them guess the answer to question 20. How many of them would you expect to get the answer correct?

Q3 These four cards are put down in random order:

(a) How many different ways of doing this are there?

(b) What is the probability that the black and the white cards are next to one another?

(c) What is the probability that the black and white cards are not next to one another?

Q4 As part of their construction course students are expected to complete two practical tasks: one has to be chosen from tasks A, B and C, the second must be chosen from tasks D and E. The choice of the first task does not affect the choice of the second task. How many different combinations of tasks could be chosen?

Q5 In a survey of 100 students, 40 say they own a desktop PC only, 25 own a laptop only and 15 own both. What is the probability that a student chosen at random:

(a) Owns both a laptop and a PC?

(b) Owns a laptop or a PC (or both)?

(c) Owns neither a laptop nor a PC?

Q6 A lecturer keeps a record of students' attendance and punctuality over the course of a term. Attendance is 100% and the figures for lateness are given in the following table:

Late	On time	Total
26	299	325

(a) Based on this information, what is the probability that a student chosen at random arrives late to a lecture?

(b) In a class of 25, how many students would you expect to arrive on time to a lecture?

Q7 The ethnic origin of applicants and enrolled students at a college are recorded and the following charts presented at a staff meeting:

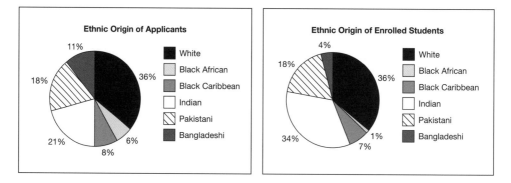

(a) What is the probability that an applicant chosen at random is Black Caribbean?

(b) If an enrolled student is selected at random, from which ethnic group are they most likely to come?

(c) Applicants from which ethnic group are most likely to go on to enrol as students at the college?

Q8 Students organise a raffle to raise money for charity. 1000 tickets are sold altogether, 700 to students at the college and 300 to staff. Nick buys 5 tickets and Navdip does not buy any. Complete the following sentences by inserting one of the words certain, impossible, likely, unlikely:

(a) It is .... that Nick will win first prize.

(b) It is .... that Navdip will win first prize.

(c) It is .... that a member of staff will win first prize.

(d) It is .... that a student will win first prize.

(e) It is .... that either a student or a member of staff will win first prize.

Q9 Each day, Yusuf decides how to travel to work. He can cycle, drive or catch the bus. The probability that he cycles is 2/3. The probability that he catches the bus is 1/6.

(a) What is the probability that he does not cycle?

(b) What is the probability that he drives?

(c) Yusuf attends college for 5 days a week and for 39 weeks of the year. Assuming he doesn't miss any days, how many times would you expect him to cycle to college during the year?

Q10 In Berlin, students will be given a choice on the second day of an activity. In the morning they have a choice between:

- a museum;
- a city tour;
- an art gallery;
- shopping.

In the afternoon they have a choice between:

- a zoo;
- a shopping centre;
- a cinema;
- a tour of a football stadium.

The choice of the morning activity does not affect the choice of the afternoon activity.

How many different combinations of activities are possible?

Q11 Some students asked 50 people to guess the distance between two points. This table shows the results:

Distance in metres	Frequencies
13.00–13.99	2
14.00–14.99	5
15.00–15.99	9
16.00–16.99	14
17.00–17.99	10
18.00–18.99	8
19.00–19.99	2

Estimate the probability that the next person asked will guess a distance of between 16 and 18 metres.

Q12 A bag contains some yellow balls and some red balls.

If the ratio of the yellow balls to the red balls is 5:6

(a) What is the minimum total number of balls in the bag?

(b) There are actually 20 yellow balls. How many red balls are there?

Michelle puts yellow and red balls in a different bag. She says to Ruth, 'the ratio of yellow balls to red balls is still 5:6 but there are 5 more red balls than yellow balls'.

(c) What number of each colour are there in the bag?

(d) If a ball is picked at random from this bag, what is the probability that it is red?

Q13 The cards used in a child's game have either a square, a triangle, a circle or a star printed on them.

The table shows the probabilities of choosing the shapes.

Outcome	Square	Triangle	Circle	Star
Probability	0.2	0.35		0.3

(a) Complete the table.

The cards are either red or blue. There are three times as many blue cards as red cards.

(b) What is the probability that the card drawn is red?

A SUMMARY OF KEY POINTS

In this chapter you have learnt how to:

> **use appropriate methods, operations and tools to explore a situation and solve problems;**

> **use appropriate reasoning, strategies and techniques to solve problems;**

> **apply appropriate knowledge of probability and skills in probability;**

> **assess your own level of understanding in the context of probability.**

REFERENCES AND FURTHER READING REFERENCES AND FURTHER READING

There are few books specifically targeted at probability. Most GCSE textbooks written for the higher tier of entry will cover the probability content.
However, some useful sources of further reading at an appropriate level are:
Cooke, H., Houssart, J. and Mason, J. (2001) *Passport to Numeracy*. Buckingham: Open University Press.
Mooney, C., Ferrie, L., Fox, S., Hansen, A. and Wrathmell, R. (2009) *Primary Mathematics: Knowledge and Understanding*. (4th ed.) Exeter: Learning Matters.

Websites
www.nrich.maths.org.uk
www.cimt.plymouth.ac.uk
www.bbc.co.uk/gcsebitesize
www.bbc.co.uk/revision

Extracts from the Minimum Core Numeracy Framework

The central theme of this book has been the minimum core for numeracy. To enable you to link to your own personal and professional development, extracts from the Minimum Core, Part B – Personal Numeracy Skills (pages 35–39) are provided below:

PART B – PERSONAL NUMERACY SKILLS

COMMUNICATION	Personal Numeracy skills for teaching and professional life.
Communicate with others about numeracy in an open and supportive manner	This requires trainee teachers to communicate about numeracy in a manner that supports open discussion.
	Using discussion about numeracy should include: • communicating numeracy concepts, skills and information with individuals and groups • developing own and others' understanding of numeracy concepts and skills • promoting enquiry and sharing of numeracy ideas • promoting reflection as a community.
Assess own and other people's understanding	This requires trainee teachers to be able to assess their own, and others' understanding.
	Assessment techniques should include: • personal review and reflection • peer assessment • questioning for understanding • recognising and analysing misconceptions • formal assessment methods such as written tests and observations.
Express yourself clearly and accurately	This requires trainee teachers to be able to: • communicate number concepts clearly and effectively • use the language of numeracy accurately.

	Appropriate communication should include: • using logical sequences and making connections • structuring material • use of debate around justification and/or argument • using illustrations, analogy and examples that consider real life contexts • accurate use of taxonomy such as equality signs • correct use of language such as for 2D and 3D shapes • appropriateness concerning accuracy and estimation.
Communicate about numeracy in a variety of ways that suit and support the intended audience, and recognise such use by others	This requires trainee teachers to be able to: • recognise differences in language needs • formulate and provide appropriate responses • recognise appropriate use of communication about numeracy by others.
	Appropriate approaches should include: • checking how the information is received and explaining terms or modifying language appropriately • adapting delivery according to level, needs and prior knowledge of the audience • using pitch, pace, stress and intonation to reinforce meaning • using non-verbal cues • interpreting non-verbal cues of others • listening to the audience to identify the range of their numeracy related vocabulary • identifying errors in terminology and correcting them.
Use appropriate techniques to reinforce oral communication, check how well the information is received and support the understanding of those listening	This requires trainee teachers to be able to use language and other forms of representation to: • reinforce oral communication of numeracy concepts and skills

<table>
<tr>
<td></td>
<td>

• check how well the information is received
• support the understanding of those listening.

</td>
</tr>
<tr>
<td></td>
<td>

Appropriate techniques should include:

• provision of notes, summaries and examples
• repeating, rephrasing and summarising
• employing a range of questioning techniques
• requesting feedback and responding appropriately
• asking for a summary of information given
• the use of visual aids including still and moving images and animations, equipment and artefacts
• the use of information and communications technology.

</td>
</tr>
<tr>
<td>

PROCESSES

</td>
<td>

Personal Numeracy skills for teaching and professional life.

</td>
</tr>
<tr>
<td>

Use strategies to make sense of a situation requiring the application of numeracy

</td>
<td>

This requires trainee teachers to be able to identify familiar and unfamiliar contexts within the scope of their professional role that can be analysed and explored through numeracy.

</td>
</tr>
<tr>
<td></td>
<td>

This requires trainee teachers to be able to explore and represent situations in a range of forms.

Range of forms should include:

• diagrams, charts and graphs
• tables
• models.

</td>
</tr>
<tr>
<td></td>
<td>

This requires trainee teachers to be able to employ appropriate methods, operations and tools, including ICT to explore a situation.

Appropriate methods should include:

• making connections between the current situation and those they have met previously

</td>
</tr>
</table>

	• employing systematic methods • breaking the problem down.
Process and analyse data	This requires trainee teachers to be able to use appropriate reasoning, strategies and techniques when tackling problems. Appropriate reasoning should include: • using knowledge of related problems • planning ahead • looking for and examining patterns • making and beginning to justify conjectures • exploring effects of varying values • working logically • taking account of constraints and assumptions • reasoning inductively and deductively • using feedback.
	Appropriate strategies should include: • using diagrams, charts and graphs • calculating accurately, using a calculator where appropriate • using notation accurately • recording methods, results and conclusions • estimating, approximating and checking working.
Use generic content knowledge and skills	This requires trainee teachers to be able to apply appropriate knowledge and skills to problem solving processes.
	Appropriate knowledge and skills should be relevant to trainee teachers in their role and could include: • understanding positive and negative numbers of any size • carrying out calculations with numbers of any size • understanding and using equivalences between fractions, decimals and per-centages • calculating with fractions • calculating with decimals to a given number of decimal places • using and calculating with ratio and proportion

	• working with unknown values and variables • having a knowledge of and using the properties of common 2D and 3D shapes • creating and interpreting 2D representations of 3D objects • working with area, perimeter, volume and capacity of shapes • interpreting and using rates of change • working with money, metric and, where appropriate, imperial units • using conversion tables and scales • manipulating discrete and continuous data • understanding and creating frequency diagrams, pie charts and scatter diagrams • understanding likelihood or probability • using the probability scale from 0 to 1. A range of note-taking techniques should be included. For example, linear and diagrammatic styles.
Make decisions concerning content knowledge and skills	This requires trainee teachers to be able to assess their own level of understanding of the areas of numeracy required.
	This requires trainee teachers to be able to identify means of addressing their own learning needs.
	Appropriate approaches to dealing with gaps in personal knowledge should include: • calling upon subject experts for support • using professional development opportunities • using reference material including books and the Internet.
Understand the validity of different methods	This requires trainee teachers to be able to assess the validity of different methods when applied to particular situations.

	Different methods should include: • the use of calculators • formal and informal methods of calculation • graphical methods • the use of ICT tools, such as spreadsheets.
Consider accuracy, efficiency and effectiveness when solving problems and reflect on what has been learnt	This requires trainee teachers to be able to: • consider whether alternative strategies may have helped or been better • identify more efficient methods when they are presented • consider the impact of assumptions made and the appropriateness and accuracy of results and conclusions • assess the strength of empirical evidence • understand the difference between evidence and proof.
Make sense of data	This requires trainee teachers to be able to make connections between the situation currently being studied and ones they have met before. This requires trainee teachers to be able to: • put forward convincing arguments based on findings and make general statements • relate findings to the original context.
Select appropriate format and style for communicating findings	This requires trainee teachers to be able to: • communicate findings in a range of forms • talk about their findings.

Answers to key questions

2. Skills audit

1 4.05 m² – calculation is (6 × 0.9) – (1.1 × 0.9) – (0.4 × 0.9)

2 Answer × 13.5 × 1.175 should be 4.05 × 13.5 × 1.175 = £64.24

3 Length 8.5 m and width 6 m

4 Total area = 60 m²; area of tables = 24 × 0.5² = 6 m²; practical area = 60 – 6 = 54 m².
   Ratio = 54 : 6 i.e. 9 : 1

5 –4°

6 Range

7 (a) £1987
   (b) books, photocopying, equipment

8 Textbooks → 10, stopwatches → 5, name cards → 15 reams of paper → 20

9 Friday 23 November

10 141%

11 Either 800 × 2 → £16 or 780 × 2 → £15.60

12 (d)

13 (a) (i) No
        (ii) No
        (iii) Yes
        (iv) No
        (v)   No

   (b) For example,
        (i)   males spend on average more time on computers/internet than females do;
        (ii) females on average spend more time shopping and socialising than men do;
        (iii) males on average do more paid work than females.

14 Females: 8.625, i.e. 8½ hrs. Males: 7.9 i.e. 8 hrs

15 ICT 79.7%, Literacy 78.3%, Numeracy 79.5%

16 £30.76

17 (a) 6hr 45 min
   (b) 10.15
   (c) 432km – accept between 430 and 440km

18 12

19 £5 × 6 + £10 = £40

20 0.7 times 70

21 8.75 i.e. 9 amps

22 647 miles

3. Number

1 −1°C

2 (a) £1835
   (b) books, photocopying, equipment

3

	For a class of 18
Textbooks	12
Stopwatches	6
Name cards	18
Reams of paper	24

4 £24

5

	Retention rate (%)
ICT	83.4
Literacy	89.0
Numeracy	82.1

6 £45.90

7 908.8 km

8 £24

9 0.7 times 70

10 (i)   incorrect – correct answer = 18.4
   (ii) incorrect – correct answer = ¾ hour
   (iii) incorrect – correct answer = 0.08
   (iv) incorrect – correct answer = 53,407

11 (a) 1 kg or 1000 g
   (b) 417 g

12 (a) 4.8 cm
   (b) 3.1 cm

13 619 words = 2.19 pages i.e. 2 pages

14 £104.79

15 (a)
16 (a) 2 : 1
   (b) 231/700 = 0.33
   (c) 44/175 = 33%

17 £165

18 (a) 69 : 167
   (b) 14.4%
   (c) 28/65 = 0.43

19 (a) £462
 (b) £11.48

20 (a) A
 (b) D
 (c) £77
 (d) 40p

21 −3°C

22 Box of 80

23 (a) 12 45
 (b) 40.2
 (c) rough calculation for (a) (6 × 5) ÷ 2)
   rough calculation for (b) (3 × 5 × 25) ÷ 10

24 3.5, 1.7

25 (a) 13.6%
 (b) 439.5 ml

26 £127.24

27 (a) 3256
 (b) 30.2%
 (c) No – 1089 is only 33.5% of the total intake of 3256

4. Algebra

1 (a) £217
 (b) £575
 (c) $(115p + 0.6(q − 80p))$

2 (a) 22 mph
 (b) 45.5 m/s

3 6.8 m × 5.3 m

4 (c)

5 £47

6 (a) 2200 watts
 (b) 4 amps

7 4

8

	A	B	C	D
1	1	1	1	3
2	2	4	8	14
3	3	7	21	31
4	4	10	40	54
5	5	13	65	83
6	6	16	96	118
7	7	19	133	159
8	8	22	176	206

9 (a) (i)   59°F
     (ii) 10°C
     (iii) 37.8°C
   (b) (i)   77°F
     (ii) 60°C
     (iii) −40°C

10

	True/false	Which law?
$a + b = b + a$	√	commutative
$(a + b) + c = a + (b + c)$	√	associative
$a \times b = b \times a$	√	commutative
$a - b = b - a$	X	
$(a - b) - c = a - (b - c)$	X	
$a \times (b \times c) = a \times b + b \times c$	X	
$(a \div b) \div c = a \div (b \div c)$	X	
$(a - b) \times c = a \times c - b \times c$	√	distributive
$(a \times b) \times c = a \times (b \times c)$	√	associative

11 (i)   14.5
   (ii) 20
   (iii) 6

12 130 minutes

13 22

14 56.3 i.e. 56

15 2051

16 1210, −0.99

17 (a) 4, 2, 5, 8, 4
   (b) The sequence repeats, 4, 2, 5, 8, 4 so that every 4th number is 8. 500 is a multiple of 4 so that the 500th term must be 8
   (c) Either 112, 56, 28 or 53, 56, 28, or 22, 25, 28

18 (a) $\dfrac{n(n + 1)}{2}$

   (b) 210

19 300

20 (a)

Number of tickets	1	2	3	4
Cost in £	28	53	78	103

   (b) $(n \times 25) + 3$
   (c) 5

5. Shape and space

1 (a) 11
   (b) (i)   C
       (ii) A
       (iii) B

2 For example:

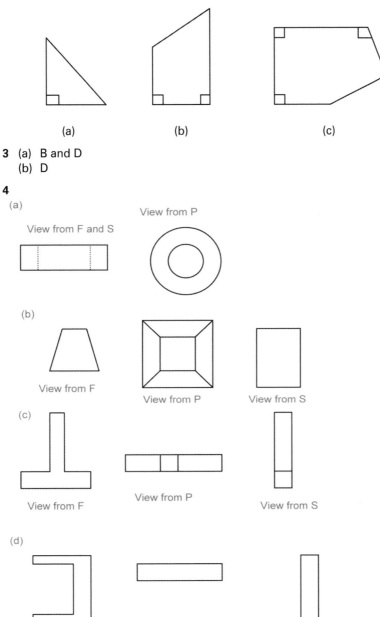

         (a)   (b)   (c)

3 (a) B and D
   (b) D

4

(a)

View from F and S

View from P

(b)

View from F

View from P   View from S

(c)

View from F

View from P

View from S

(d)

View from F   View from P   View from S

5 $p = 140°, q = 40°, r = 30°$

6 $a = 70°$, (angles in a triangle add to 180°), $b = 65°$ (corresponding angles)

7 $a = 89°, b = 58°$

8

	Sides		Diagonals	Parallel sides	
Quadrilateral	Four equal sides	Two different pairs of equal sides	Equal diagonals	Two pairs of parallel sides	Only one pair of parallel sides
Square	✓		✓	✓	
Rectangle		✓	✓	✓	
Rhombus	✓		✓	✓	
Parallelogram		✓		✓	
Trapezium					✓
Kite		✓			

9 (a) 75°
   (b) 37°
   (c) 35°
   (d) 70°

10 57°

11 111°

12 (a) isosceles
   (b) $x = 43°$ $y = 43°$

13 (a) B, F, H
   (b) C

14 Cuboid – a cube would have all three edges the same length

15

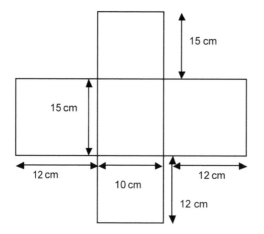

6. Measures

1 52.5 : 60 = 7:8

2 2 km

3 (a) 22°C
　　(b) 125

4 6.7 m/s

5 (a) 5.8 m³
　　(b) £156.60

6 21 cm²

7 0.54 m³

8 (a) 72 cm
　　(b) (i)　144 cm
　　　　(ii)　36 cm
　　(c) 648 cm²

9 15

10 (a) 312
　　(b) 44 cm

11 (a) 17.05 m
　　(b) 3.41 m²
　　(c) £15 – the total area = 6.82 m²

12 (a) 5.6 km
　　(b) 52.5 mins

13　18.5 m

14 8.4 m, 5.2 m

15 Wednesday 19 December

16 (a) 3.5 hours
　　(b) 13.15

17 477 miles

18 13.05

19 7.8m³

7. Handling data

1 Range

2 Females: 8.625 hours ie 8½ hours, males: 7.9 hours i.e. 8 hours

3 (a)

Width measurement in cm	Frequency F	Midpoint X	F x X
13.00–13.99	1	13.5	13.5
14.00–14.99	1	14.5	14.5
15.00–15.99	3	15.5	46.5
16.00–16.99	7	16.5	115.5
17.00–17.99	5	17.5	87.5
18.00–18.99	2	18.5	37
19.00–19.99	1	19.5	19.5
Total	20		334

    (b) 16.7
    (c) 1.67

4 (a) Scotland
    (b) Wales
    (c) Northern Ireland

5 (a) No
    (b) Yes
    (c) No

6 (a) 90°
    (b)

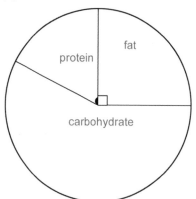

7 66

8 64

9 (a) 35 minutes

    (b) 115.4 minutes = 1 hour 55 minutes

10 (a) 167
    (b) £2595.40

11 1/12

12 (a) Females over 60 should read 8 not 7
    (b) 44
    (c) 7/39

13 (a) 73
    (b) 52%
    (c) 0.6%

14 (a) 1
    (b) 84

15 For example,
    (i) males spend on average more time per week on computers/internet than females do;
    (ii) on average men and women spend the same length of time per week socialising;
    (iii) females on average do 1.5 hours less paid work per week than males.

8. Probability

1 (a) 0.6
    (b) 0.37
    (c) 0.12

2 (a) 0.2
    (b) 6
    (c) 20

3 (a) 24
    (b) 12/24
    (c) 12/24

4 6

5 (a) 0.15
    (b) 0.8
    (c) 0.2

6 (a) 0.08
    (b) 23

7 (a) 0.8 or 8/100 or 2/25
    (b) White
    (c) Indian

8 (a) unlikely
    (b) impossible
    (c) unlikely
    (d) likely
    (e) certain

9 (a) 1/3
    (b) 1/6
    (c) 130

10 16

11 0.48 or 24/50

12 (a) 11
    (b) 24
    (c) 25 yellow and 30 red
    (d) 30/55 = 6/11

13 (a) All the probabilities must add to 1. 0.2 + 0.35 + 0.3 = 0.85. Therefore probability for the circle cards is 0.15

(b) $\frac{1}{4}$ (there are 4 'parts' in total, 3 'parts' of the total are blue so 1 'part' is red)

Index